Theobald Wolfe Tone and the Irish Nation

C. Desmond Greaves

with Prefaces by

Anthony Coughlan and
Peter Berresford Ellis

THE FULCRUM PRESS
DUBLIN 1991

First edition published 1961; Second edition 1989;
Third edition published in 1991 by
The Fulcrum Press,
43 East Essex Street,
Dublin 2,
Ireland

ISBN 1-872993-02-8

History — Ireland — Wolfe Tone — United Irishmen

Cover Design:
Typesetting: The Fulcrum Press

Contents

The Memory of the Dead

Who fears to speak of 'Ninety-eight?
Who blushes at the name?
When cowards mock the patriot's fate
Who hangs his head for shame?
He's all a knave or half a slave
Who slights his country thus,
But true men, like you, men,
Will fill your glass with us.

We drink the memory of the brave,
The faithful and the few,
Some lie far off beyond the wave,
Some sleep in Ireland too;
All, all are gone, but still lives on
The fame of those who died,
And true men, like you, men,
Remember them with pride.

Some on the shores of distant lands
Their weary hearts have laid,
And by the stranger's heedless hands
Their lonely graves were made;
But though their clay be far away,
Beyond the Atlantic foam,
In true men, like you, men,
Their spirit's still at home.

The dust of some is Irish earth,
Among their own they rest;
And that same land that gave them birth
Has caught them to her breast;
And we will pray that from their clay
Full many a race may start
Of true men, like you, men,
To play as brave a part.

They rose in dark and evil days
To free their native land
And kindled then a living blaze
That nothing shall withstand;
Alas, that might should conquer right,
They fell and passed away
But true men, like you, men,
Are plenty here today.

Then here's their memory, let it be
To us a guiding light
To cheer our fight for liberty
And teach us to unite!
Though good and ill be Ireland's still,
Though sad as theirs your fate,
Yet true men, be you, men,
Like those of 'Ninety-eight.

J. K.Ingram

Preface to the 1991 Edition

Anthony Coughlan

HISTORICAL "REVISIONISM" AND TONE

The late C. Desmond Greaves had thought of expanding this study of Wolfe Tone and Irish nationality before his death in 1988. Eye-trouble among other things prevented him. But in the early eighties he wrote asking me to secure for him such relevant new books on the 1790s as had appeared since this work was first published in 1963.

At the time there was not much. G.C.Bolton's study of *The Passing of the Act of Union* (Oxford 1966) was important. R.B.McDowell's *Ireland in the Age of Imperialism and Revolution* (Oxford 1979) was full of eccentric detail. Marianne Elliott's *Partners in Revolution: The United Irishmen and France* (New Haven and London 1982) contained new material on the French dimension of the period. But historians on the whole seemed to have neglected the United Irishmen. As the so-called "revisionist" movement in Irish history-writing was by then in full spate, one had the impression that perhaps the 1790s, when Protestant, Catholic and Dissenter had united for a while under the common name of Irishmen, might not be the most fruitful decade for revisionism.

I recall being present in 1963 at the meeting of the Irish Historical Society at which Professors Moody and McDowell of Trinity College announced that they were undertaking the editing of everything Tone wrote — autobiography, pamphlets, letters, the lot. There was a flourish of trumpets in the press at the time. In the early 1960s Establishment Ireland still felt sufficiently positive about republicanism to wish to honour the Tone bicentenary. But in the years since, republicanism, 18th century or later, has been out of fashion. One reason is the Northern troubles; another the need to play down the value of Ireland's struggle for independent statehood so as to justify integration with the Common Market and a quasi-federal European Union based upon it.

Nearly thirty years after the announcement of the Moody-McDowell project, the non-appearance of Tone's works — above all the

1

magnificent *Autobiography*, which is in Trinity College Library — has assumed the dimensions of an academic scandal. There has never been a complete edition of the *Autobiography*. His son's edition of 1826 omitted some one-tenth of the material for various reasons. Its eventual appearance will be a publishing event.

The bicentenary of the French Revolution and the advent of the 1990s have stimulated new research on the United Irishmen period. Revisionism could no longer ignore the challenge of the 1790s. Its emphasis has been predictable. Whereas traditional nationalist historiography emphasised the achievement of political unity among Protestants and Catholics in the 1790s as having been a good thing, revisionism tends to denigrate that, to play down the extent of cross-religious cooperation, play up incidents of religious sectarianism, and explicitly or implicitly write an apologia for Dublin Castle and English Government policy at the time.

Taking their cue from Frank MacDermot's 1939 biography of Tone, revisionist historians have subscribed for example to the concept of a Wexford "sectarian bloodbath", with reference to the 1798 rebellion in that county.* Sectarianism of course existed. Many people had been robbed of their land by Protestant landlords a century before. Some remembered and sought revenge. But the good historian will recognise the political achievement of Tone and the United Irishmen, while understanding what people can get up to in the turmoil of events. Tone himself wrote at the time that he "apprehended every excess from the just resentment of the people." Dr. Kevin Whelan has recently shown that the Wexford rebels scrupulously respected the Quakers; they left good landlords alone while avenging themselves on bad; and they were of course themselves in the main led by Protestants. He writes: "The sectarian explanation, in which the Scullabogue and Wexford bridge massacres loom large, was essentially a propagandist creation, a necessary scapegoating of the beaten rebels and a political ploy to detach Presbyterian Ulster from radicalism."**

Much work still needs to be done on the Defenders. Revisionism implies that they were anti-Protestant sectarians. Doubtless their

---

* v. L.M.Cullen, *The Emergence of Modern Ireland 1600-1900*, London 1981, p.218
**In Hugh Gough and David Dickson, *Ireland and the French Revolution*, Dublin 1990, p.156. See also Whelan in P. O'Flanagan, ed., *Rural Ireland, Modernisation and Change 1600-1900*, Cork 1987.

character varied from place to place, but many had sworn the United Irishman oath and took seriously the republican ideal of cross-religious political unity. Dr. Emmet O' Connor sees Defenderism as a form of rural trade unionism and the Defenders' participation in the 1798 Rising as making that event "the first and greatest trade union revolt in Irish history."*

REVISIONISM'S ATTACK ON TONE

In Dr. Marianne Elliott's biography, *Wolfe Tone, Prophet of Irish Independence* (New Haven and London, 1989) revisionism makes a frontal assault on Tone himself. This book, though it contains interesting new material, is revealing of the ideological thrust of much Irish revisionist history-writing. This might properly be termed "neo-unionist", although its exponents sometimes claim to be writing value-free history. As Dr. Elliott's book is likely to remain the most consulted work on Tone until the *Autobiography* is published and the man can, so to say, speak for himself, its tendentiously hostile character is worth noting. This possibly stems from the author's lack of sympathy with the ideal of an independent All-Ireland Republic which Tone and his fellow-Protestants came to adopt in the 1790s, and which still remains unattained. Doubtless it is difficult to write a sympathetic biography of a political figure if one does not to some extent share his views. A critical study does not have to be a whitewash, but Dr. Elliott writes of Tone as if he were a proto-Provisional.

She reveals her political standpoint when she writes of Tone's "tendency to raise Irish independence from a domestic squabble to a key role in a new international order." A "domestic squabble" implies that the matter had little to do with English Government policy. The cumulative effect of her patronising and pejorative characterisations shows how out of sympathy she is with her subject. Thus Tone's republicanism was an "accident of character." He was "a young Whig careerist," "no democrat," "temporarily unhinged in his mind," "with an inflated sense of honour," "not an original thinker." She says that his "thought-processes were simplistic." She refers to "Tone's shibboleths — England, aristocracy and privilege."

In contrast to C. Desmond Greaves's book, which shows how Tone's

---

*Emmet O'Connor, *Labour History of Waterford*, Waterford 1989, p. 370

3

politics and character developed in interaction with the evolving circumstances of his time, Dr. Elliott's lack of sympathy with her subject — perhaps also her political inexperience — vitiate her ability to explain adequately what drove Tone and many others to embrace republicanism in the 1790s. She writes as if this step were due to mental aberration. She scarcely refers to the policy or motivation of the contemporary English Government, despite its obvious relevance. She has a sentence stating that from as early as 1792 Prime Minister Pitt was aiming at a legislative union of Ireland and Britain, but leaves this vital matter in the air. No reference for it is given in the extensive notes.* The impact of French developments on Ireland before 1791, two years from the Revolution's commencement, is scarcely mentioned, though Tone had much to say of them. This leads to a playing-down of the radicalising effect of the Revolution on the Northern Dissenters. She gives no impression of the panic induced in the landlord class by events in France, or of the threat to their privileges which lay in Protestant-Catholic unity — and which led Pitt to see in a legislative union the best defence of aristocracy and landlordism in both islands.

APOLOGIA FOR DUBLIN CASTLE

Again in contrast to Greaves's treatment, Dr. Elliott fails to make clear that from the mid-1790s onward the Dublin Castle administration, relying on the Ascendancy landlord class and supported by the English Government which appointed the Irish Executive, set out as a matter of deliberate policy to provoke isolated and premature uprisings among the population, which might more easily be crushed before French help arrived. Her apologetic treatment of Government actions means that in her chapter entitled "Witch Hunt" it is hard to tell who are the witches and who is doing the hunting. Thus in one paragraph she writes "That winter a war was waged by the Defenders", implying that the Catholics were the aggressors. But the very next paragraph states "There was an element of self-defence in Defender efforts to arm themselves," implying that they were the objects of aggression. Failure

---

*E.M.Johnston, *Ireland in the Eighteenth Century*, Dublin 1974, p.175, quotes Pitt as writing to Lord Lieutenant Westmoreland in November 1792: "The idea of the present fermentation gradually bringing both parties to think of a union with this country, has long been in my mind. The admission of the Catholics to a share in the suffrage would not then be dangerous." Johnston also quotes evidence to indicate that Pitt was thinking of a legislative union as far back as 1785.

4

to judge on such an important matter, so crucial to understanding the politics of the time, is scarcely testimony to academic balance.

Dr. Elliott's reluctance to criticise the actions of the Dublin Castle authorities during the 1790s — so typical of the ideological parti pris of the Irish "revisionist" school — leads her to resort to sociological abstraction about "riots revealing popular alienation from authority and a breakdown of the forces of social control." She criticises the United Irishmen for "whipping up discontent" with handbills, ballads, squibs and broadsheets, and implicitly puts this on the same plane as the discontent resulting from the dragooning, pitchcapping, flogging and hanging by the Government forces, that were primarily responsible for the aforementioned "riots". She refers vaguely to Defender "disturbances" after 1791, but leaves the reader in the dark as to what they amounted to or what caused them. Her index has no reference to Orangeism or the Orange Order. A passing reference to the Order's foundation at the height of the rural disturbances leads to no consideration of Orangeism's significance as a sectarian weapon in the hands of the most reactionary landed gentry, whose use was fully encouraged by the Government. It is not surprising, in view of all this, that she pays tribute in her text to "Frank MacDermot's balanced life of Tone," although MacDermot's biography is notorious among Tone scholars for its extreme hostility to its subject and his politics.

LIQUIDATING THE HERITAGE OF THE FRENCH REVOLUTION

C. Desmond Greaves did not believe that there could be such a thing as non-partisan history — at least not when the historian is dealing with issues touching his own life and times. He held that the important thing was that the good historian be conscious of and declare his partisanship, while endeavouring honestly to "tell it as it was." He had a poor opinion of many academic historians for failing to do this and for pretending to an objectivity they in no way possessed. He regarded Irish "revisionism" as essentially an ideological apologia for contemporary Transnational Capital and the political projects it upholds, in particular the subversion of national democracy and independence through the European Community.

In today's world of giant transnational firms there exists a concerted attempt to erode the Nation State as the locus of political democracy. Whatever the problems of the international State system, it is surely valid to contend that the Nation State, either on its own or in cooperation with other States, is the principal mechanism that history has evolved for imposing democratic responsibility and social control on private capital and the disposal of society's investment surplus. Hence the hostility of modern Big Capital, which resists such controls, to national democracy and national sovereignty. It may be said that in general the erosion of these values is the political effect of the European Community, whose constitution, the Treaty of Rome, is the first in history to be drawn up exclusively in the interests of big business, without the slightest democratic element. Politically, West European integration entails the erosion of the national democracy of the Member States concerned. It may therefore be regarded as in effect an attempt to liquidate the democratic heritage of the French Revolution, with its assertion of the principle of the right of nations to self-determination. For democracy can exist normally only at the level of the national community. The reason is that it is within national communities alone that there exists sufficient solidarity, mutual identification and mutuality of interest among people as to induce minorities freely to agree to majority-rule. Upholding the independence and capacity for free cooperation of sovereign Nation States in today's world becomes therefore a struggle in defence of democracy. Participating in that struggle is the very essence of internationalism.

C.Desmond Greaves was a lifelong student of nationality problems. He believed that the most urgent task facing democrats, the Labour movement and socialists in our time is to develop an international campaign in defence of national democracy and the Nation State. He saw the European Community, and the proposed European Union developing out of it, as likely to make the national question the key issue of West European politics over the coming half-century. East European events since 1989 have shown a host of forgotten nationalities reasserting themselves. It seems very likely that the establishment of new Nation States in Europe and the Third World, so as to enable the developing national communities of those parts to relate to one another on the international scene, will be a key theme of world history for centuries to come.

Such national movements will continue to seek inspiration in the French Revolution and in the political example and doctrine of national unity of T.W.Tone, that most humanly appealing of all Ireland's political leaders. Reading C.Desmond Greaves's minor historical classic may also help Northern Protestants rediscover their progressive historical heritage, as well as encourage those who hope to see Protestants and Catholics come together politically in the Ireland of the 1990s, as their forefathers did two centuries ago.

Anthony Coughlan
Trinity College, Dublin, 1991

Preface to the 1989 Edition

Peter Berresford Ellis

There has been a small corpus of works which have shaped my thought and attitude towards an understanding of Irish history. I first encountered this little book in 1964, about a year after its first publication, and realised that here was a political assessment of Irish history of major importance. Its author's name was already known to me as the biographer of James Connolly. One of my father's family had been among the first to join the Citizens Army and I grew up with Connolly's works on my father's bookshelves. By the time I first met the author, C. Desmond Greaves (1913-1988), in 1972 I had come to recognise him as an historian and political thinker of the first water.

Wolfe Tone and the Irish Nation was first issued as a contribution to the bicentenary of the birth of Tone. It is more than fitting that it should now be reissued during the bicentenary of the French Revolution. The work is as relevant as ever it was, presenting a succinct overview of Irish history, with an exposition of the twin evils of English rule and landlordism, before coming to a consideration of the life and work of Tone. As Desmond Greaves says: ''Without a survey of that history, their significance and the significance of Tone's lifework cannot be understood.''

In a way, it is sad that the political lessons Greaves addressed to the readers in 1963 are still relevant twenty-six years later; for this indicates not only the perception of Greaves but the failure of our generation to succeed in breaking the fetters of the past.

One important relevance of this work is its very publication at a time when Irish history is under threat. We have, in recent times, witnessed the growth of a school of historians who are popularly known by the appelation of ''revisionists,'' although I would call them ''apologists for empire.'' This group has been hard at work seeking to change our perceptions of Irish history, to denigrate the struggle for self-determination and present it as the aberration of a small faction not

8

truly representative of the will of the people. The populist tradition of republicanism and the social struggle as inseparable from the national struggle has been dismissed as verging on irrelevant to the development of the modern Irish nation. Desmond Greaves was perturbed by what he saw as the growth of this movement, the attempt to make Irish history more comfortable for the English establishment and more obscure for the Irish people. This "revisionism" has been a phenomenon which has developed against the background of the current war in North-East Ulster. Its theme is that history has to be revised to negate the nationalist or republican aspects, particularly to eradicate any sign of popular support for such philosophies. It is a theme which has been joyously taken up by several Irish historians who would undoubtedly like the unfinished business of the achievement of Irish freedom to vanish in the pseudo-erudition of their inconsequential monographs and tomes.

This booklet will not sit well on any revisionist shelf.

The difference in approach by Desmond Greaves to the new "revisionist" history can best be seen in the discussion of the death of Wolfe Tone. Frank MacDermot, in *Theobald Wolfe Tone* (Macmillan, 1939) states: "that he cut his own throat is, in fact, as sure as anything in history." MacDermot (1886-1975) is now seen as one of the prototype "revisionists"; an ex-British Army officer, lawyer, banker, who was elected independent T.D. for Roscommon in 1932, made the Senate in 1938, and was a vociferous critic of Irish neutrality, leaving Ireland in 1945 to take a job with the *Sunday Times*. MacDermot's book is simply a long-sustained attack on Wolfe Tone whom it paints as "inconsistent," "full of fluctuations" and a "self-seeker" whose "fear of poverty and obscurity played a larger part than might be desired in moulding his thoughts and conduct." On a wider level: "The glorification of the Jacobins by the United Irishmen brought turbulence and bloodshed into fashion and inspired even mild and moderate men with the ferocity of panic." With such attitudes one might be tempted to dismiss MacDermot. But Greaves is a considerate and careful historian. Considering his statement: "That he (Tone) cut his own throat is, in fact, as sure as anything in history," Greaves says: "The very exaggeration of the statement shows its bias. As sure as anything in history?" Yet revisionists have seized joyously on MacDermot's bias. Dr Marianne Elliott, addressing the Liverpool Branch of the Connolly Association on March 5 this year, pronounced that he committed suicide

9

and there was no room for any other consideration. Her view of the United Irishmen, like MacDermot's views, was that they were merely a group of dilettantes and poseurs.

Yet more careful historians consider the facts. Lord Chief Justice Arthur Viscount Kilwarden (1739-1803), a supporter of the Union with Britain in 1800, who was killed on the night of the Emmet uprising, recognised that Tone's trial and death sentence by court-martial in November 1798 was illegal. He issued a writ of habeas corpus for the military to hand Tone over to civil jurisdiction. Major Sandys, the jailor, ignored this writ. The Lord Justice then gave orders for the writ to be served again by the Sheriff of Dublin with instructions for the arrest of the Provost Marshal, Major Sandys and General Craig, if the order was ignored. It was believed that the handing over of Tone to a civil court would result in his exchange, as a French citizen and one holding a commission in the French Army, for a notable English prisoner held by France. In fact steps were being taken to that effect.

When the Sheriff returned to the jail to serve the writ, he was informed that Tone had attempted to commit suicide. Since the first attempt to serve the writ of habeas corpus Tone had been held incommunicado with not even close relatives allowed to see him. After his death, a few days later, the military allowed no post mortem. To say the least, these circumstances are highly suspicious. One could possibly conclude that the military authorities, realising their prisoner was about to be taken from them by a civil court and perhaps exchanged with the French, decided to pre-empt matters and ensure his execution, disguising it as suicide. It is not beyond belief, as the track record of the English administration in Ireland demonstrates.

On the other hand, Tone had mentioned suicide some time previously — although such mention does not show any clear intention of suicide in the event of capture. Nevertheless, Tone's son accepted the suicide explanation while, at the same time, pointing out the suspicious circumstances.

Greaves comments: "It would be better to say that while nobody will ever know precisely what happened when Tone was held incommunicado by his captors after an illegal trial, there are few instances where suspicion is more justified, and historians are as entitled to record that Tone was murdered while in illegal custody, as to accept his jailors' word for it and record that he cut his own throat."

At that illegal court-martial on November 10 1798, Tone said: "I have regarded the connection between Ireland and Great Britain as the curse of the Irish nation: and I felt that while it lasted the country could never be free nor happy!''

Nearly two centuries later that statement rings out with clarity. Ireland still remains fettered to England and cannot pursue any constructive path to social democracy while those fetters remain. As Greaves says: "Separation is necessary because history has bequeathed to Ireland a set of social problems which differ from those of Britain, which no administration at Westminster, however enlightened, can possibly undertake to solve."

Today, the evils of Partition remain. James Connolly rightly saw the then proposed Partition as a betrayal of national democracy which would give rise (as it indeed has!) to a carnival of reaction that would set back the wheels of progress, destroy the unity of Irish labour and paralyze all advanced movements for as long as it endured. Partition must be ended, national democracy must be restored in Ireland before social progress can be made, for national and social freedoms are not two separate and unrelated issues but two sides of one great democratic principle, each being incomplete without the other.

That is the clear message of this study and no amount of rewriting of history, attempting to reinterpret it so that it becomes more acceptable to the Establishment, can alter the facts. Twenty-six years after its first publication, Desmond Greaves's *Wolfe Tone and the Irish Nation* still speaks with a perception, a clarity and foresight which the Irish people need more than ever before.

Peter Berresford Ellis,
"Lios na nAislingí",
July 1989

Wolfe Tone and the Irish Nation

AUTHOR'S PREFACE

This little book is offered as a contribution to the celebration of the two hundredth anniversary of the birth of Theobald Wolfe Tone, founder of Irish Republicanism and one of the most striking political leaders produced by any country in its struggle for national independence.

Its aim is to provide a summary of Tone's life, work and opinions, against the background of the emergence of Ireland as a modern nation.

No man is born great. Nor despite the adage, does anybody ever have greatness thrust upon him. It is always acquired, and at that only through the performance of actions important to society. This is so much so that it has been said that the greatest minds are irresistibly attracted towards the solution of the most important social problems; the most courageous natures, it may be added, to the performance of society's most needed deeds. In Wolfe Tone's day the needs of Irish society proclaimed themselves with such clarity that it was as if a hand was writing them on a wall. They were first separation from England, second an agrarian revolution that would give the land to the people. The greatness of Tone lay in the fact that it was he who proclaimed the means — the unity of the common people, irrespective of religious affiliations.

Some may ask why was separation from England so urgent a matter. It should be stated clearly that separation was, and is, a necessity quite apart from any reasons of national sentiment. Indeed the sentimental approach to Irish independence has always done more harm than good. Separation is necessary because history has bequeathed to Ireland a set of social problems which differ from those of Britain, which no administration at Westminster, however enlightened, can possibly undertake to solve. But to say that separation is necessary for their solution is not to claim that isolation is necessary, but merely that salvation must come from within. Indeed only after separation can

Ireland's relations with other nations be placed on a rational footing, and there need be no doubt that such a rational footing will be one of increasing cooperation.

Since the days of Tone one formerly overwhelming problem has been removed. The landlord has been all but eliminated. But he has been eliminated in the course of a costly struggle in which Ireland has lost half her population. The importance of Tone's policy of an agrarian revolution is thus measured in the price of the failure to implement it. Landlordism was abolished within the framework of the Union; had it been rooted out by the Irish people themselves Ireland's population might now stand at something like 15 millions.

But the separation Tone fought for has only partially come about. And certainly the purpose for which it was required is totally frustrated by the present arrangement. That the Irish people cannot solve their problems without a Government is obvious. It is likewise not hard to guess that they find it little easier with two of them, especially when one of them is merely an extension of the power of Westminster on to Irish soil. And to say that special circumstances within Ireland have facilitated the development of this abnormal situation is merely to say in other words that only in Ireland can the problems of Ireland be solved. The partitionist's argument is an argument against partition.

* * *

The somewhat unusual course has been adopted of presenting what Gavan Duffy called a "bird's eye view of Irish history" before coming to the life of Wolfe Tone proper. The reason for this is partly that both landlordism and the method of British rule in Ireland were so peculiar to that country, and so embedded in its past history, that without a survey of that history their significance, and the significance of Tone's lifework, cannot be understood. It is also however that in many respects the years 1770-1800 represent the great turning point of Irish history, the period when modern Ireland was born, and when forces which had been operating for hundreds of years took a new direction. Stated in general terms this generalisation means that from the invasion of Strongbow in the twelfth century to the Treaty of Limerick in 1689, the old Ireland of the clans was being worn and weakened till it was finally destroyed.

13

Slowly throughout the eighteenth century the people of Ireland formed themselves into a new pattern, a national pattern. The examples of the American and French revolutions provided the new nation with a modern consciousness of itself, and the ensuing struggle culminated in the attempt to establish the rights of man in Ireland. Though the United Irishmen were defeated their aim has been reaffirmed by every succeeding generation. It is also of interest that the rising of 1798 was the first in which the working class played an important part, and that it is that class which has been the most consistent repository of its traditions.

If Tone had died but yesterday it would be presumptuous to place him in such a broad perspective; but the two hundredth anniversary of such a patriot occupying such a key place in Irish history is adequate reason and provides the occasion for re-examining the course of that history as a whole. It is a history full of fascinating problems; sometimes it seems to have been presided over by a kind of "imp of the perverse." In the two chapters devoted to it the reader should not seek definitive answers, which the author is not qualified to give.

References are given which may help those who wish to do so to follow up their interests in greater detail. The authorities quoted are mostly those readily accessible, and no special attempt has been made to check detail against primary sources. There are many points where historians are divided and where non-specialists must judge of the probabilities for themselves. Where there should not be any division, however, is in the general picture which has been attempted. The Norman invasion led to a period of constant war over many centuries. Almost every incident in that war which was fought upon Irish soil added some fresh complexity until so tangled did the skein become that Ireland seemed faced with something insuperable. But in the midst of the feudal chaos arose new conditions of production, the growth of a national market and national consciousness; following this came the call to forget the past, to pay no more attention to differences of origin, to sweep away privileges and distinctions and to unite under the common title of Irishmen, those alone to be outlawed who refused to do this. For many centuries the Irish people had dreamed of reversing the conquest. But it could not be reversed. The old society was scattered. Then came a generation content to "live with" the conquest. Wolfe Tone was the first man to propose the reconquest of Ireland by the Irish people, something as necessary today as it was in his time, but now rather to be seen in the modern form envisaged by the insight of James Connolly.

In carrying the struggle for that reconquest forward in modern conditions certain lessons from the past seem to call for special mention. First, though the heart of that struggle must be, and can only be, in Ireland, external circumstances must always be taken into account. These are primarily the overall European or World situation, and secondly the situation within Britain, the oppressor country. The invasion and subjection of Ireland was part of a European process, and not an isolated event. Likewise the conditions which created the need for a national revolution in Ireland were those which simultaneously demanded a democatic social transformation in Britain. This is the answer given by the study of history to those who cannot see that it is impossible for democracy in Britain to have different interests from those of democracy (expressed as the demand for national independence) in Ireland. If the British democrats do not stand for Irish freedom, then they will not get the democracy they are fighting for. It is as simple as that. And there is therefore nothing contrary to good sense or realistic judgement in seeking, indeed demanding, that British democrats today support Ireland's struggle as their forefathers among the Levellers and Radicals did in the past.

Second, the Irish national struggle cannot be separated from politics. Wolfe Tone did not wage a "pure" national struggle against England, because such a "pure" national struggle is impossible. Take one example only. English interference in Ireland had strategic and economic motives. English influence was exercised through an English colony. The English colony became Irish. In becoming Irish it constituted a "garrison class." Therefore the Irish nation could only be freed through a class struggle.

It is no use mincing words in these matters. Wolfe Tone was an Irish republican politician of consummate skill and his works are full of class judgements. Moreover, not only did he wage a class struggle in Ireland, he understood the interplay of class forces in France and England as well — no mean accomplishment, but one that could well be emulated. He was essentially practical, and anything that affected the outcome, that he would take into account.

Finally, every age has its own limitations and opportunities. History can never he formed out of disembodied ideas. It can only come out of what has gone before, now for ever untouchable except by future

15

action. The secret of every great revolutionary is the ability to grasp what is essential in his own age, the need given by past events, the opportunity provided by present circumstances. That is to say the successful revolutionary is not an artist, dependent on some flash of intuition to teach him what to do. On the contrary he is a scientist, concerned with what is before him, what it is composed of, and what it can be made into. Facts are unalterably facts until human action is brought to bear on them; then new facts arise out of them. It is impossible to stress too emphatically that Tone's political successes were due to his possessing the sense of scientific realism to an extraordinary degree; and the ultimate disappointment of his hopes, that is to say the postponement of their realisation beyond his achievable life-span, was due to the simple fact that history itself withdrew the opportunity it had offered before Tone's brilliant skill had sufficed to make avail of it.

C. Desmond Greaves
London, 1 June, 1963

1

The Conquest

It is one of of his strongest titles to the name of genius that James Connolly grasped the importance of the old Irish social system for the modern working class. In his preface to *Labour in Irish History*[1] he urged a "reconsideration and more analytical study of the laws and social structure of Ireland before the English invasion." He complained that attempts had been made to explain Gaelic institutions in terms of feudal and capitalist conceptions that did not fit them at all. He then suggested that the discoveries of the great American anthropologist Lewis Morgan[2] would prove "the key that will yet unlock the secrets of our native civilisation."

The great contribution made by Morgan was his establishment of the importance of the kinship group (*gens, kin*) as the essential unit of ancient society, not only in Europe but throughout the world. Previously sociologists had looked at the past from the standpoint of modernity, seeking in it private property, classes and their concomitant the territorial state. These did not always exist and for our purpose it should be noted neither did the nation, nor the concept of nationality. The fundamental principle of ancient society was kinship. With that principle, and to the degree that it survived, went democracy, personal independence within a framework of co-operation, and a set of social relations hard to envisage today and only explicable on that principle.

That ancient Irish society was based on kinship has been amply established today. During the period of the conquest, the system of septs and clans described by many writers had been subjected to immense stresses, and considerable modification had taken place in the old institutions. It was easy to imagine the new basis might be feudal but for one thing, namely the common ownership of land by the sept.[3] But recent work has shown that the old system before the conquest must have started from a form of society similar to the kinship societies

17

of Gaul, ancient Germany, Italy and Greece.[4] It is from the last country that most information is available and Professor George Thomson has strikingly explained the growth of kinship society in that country and its transition to a territorial state.[5]

Prendergast in his *Cromwellian Settlement of Ireland* compared the state of Ireland when Strongbow landed in the twelfth century to that which the Romans found in Gaul 1200 years previously.[6] This may be true in general principle, but it must not be concluded from it that there was some type of universal Celtic civilisation which was broken up by the Romans in Gaul and by the Normans in Ireland. None of these societies were static and both the Romans and the Normans were descended from tribes organised along lines similar to those of the Irish and the Gauls. Tribal society, as it is usually called, shows great variety, and each period in each country has its own peculiarities. In Ireland where it survived so long it is particularly dangerous to make easy generalisations.

STARTING POINT

The starting point of evolution in Ireland as elsewhere must have resembled that described by Morgan. The *gens** or kinship group consisted of the community of all persons who could presume descent from a common ancestor in the male line. Marriage must he outside the *gens*, hence there must always be more than one *gens*, and the children belong to the *gens* of the father. It is sometimes said that each *gens* was composed of families, but Morgan stresses that this is not accurate. It was composed of their males and unmarried females; a wife remained a member of her original *gens* though she joined her husband's family. To do otherwise would be to destroy the whole principle of kinship, which was as fixed and unalterable as legal title to property became in a later age.

For the kinship group was the unit of social ownership. In the early days all but strictly personal property was vested in it. Later it held the land only, though movable property was inherited within it. In general arable was given out among the families by lot each year, but grazing remained common.

As far as political organisation existed, the *gens* was the unit, decisions being taken democratically at meetings of the entire adult kindred, or

---

*The word used in ancient Rome.

through representative councils. The same principle applied to the affairs of groups of *gentes* and the larger associations of a tribal character, as also to the positions of chieftancy, kingship and war leader.

In matters of law, since there was no state with courts, police and prisons, disputes were settled between kindred and kindred. Responsibility for enforcing justice lay on the kindred of the victim. In such a society there was fierce loyalty at the heart of each kinship group. Every member of the kindred must fight even to the death for a kinsman, but his obligation did not extend to every "countryman" even if the term had any meaning to him.

According to T.A. Jackson[7] the counterpart of the Roman family is to be found in a somewhat more complex form in the ancient Irish *fine*. According to Dineen a number of *finte* (more precisely no doubt parts of *finte*) formed a *cineál*[8] whose name derives from the word *cinim* (I am born) just as *gens* is connected with *(g) natus* (born).* On this explanation *cineál* was once the name for the Irish kinship group although in recent times the word sept is more familiar. A number of kinship groups would form a clan. Both clan and sept are borrowed directly or indirectly from Latin, and must have come into use after the introduction of Christianity. Some Irish scholars prefer to use the word kin to describe the Irish *gens* or kinship group and so avoid the complexities of changing nomenclature during the long evolution of Irish society.[4]

CHANGES

It is to this evolution that we must now turn attention. The Irish family household or *fine* was a complex structure comprising several generations. As its wealth and productivity increased it found accommodation for a few slaves, serfs or wage-workers. The family held its share of the sept lands in common and shared the product in accordance with well-defined rules of precedence, theoretically based

---

*The idea of blood relationship runs through all these words, and indeed in English, where the corresponding word to *gens* is *kin*, there is an old word *kindle*, to bring forth young. *Cineál* was *cenel*, or *cenedl* in Old Irish and is present in Welsh too, where it gives us the modern word *cenedlaethol*, which means national.[9] The terminology of kinship society abounds in the name of modern institutions, showing how universal it was. We get the word nation from *natus* (born), the word kingdom is really *kin-ing-dom* (*ing* meaning son) and harks back to the forgotten days when the king was the elected son of the people.

S0036926

on the generations of which it was composed. It was the economic unit of old Irish society. Its evolution tended to a position where the people were divided between bond and free.[7] As a number of *finte* were united in a sept, and a number of septs into a *clann*, so a number of *clanna* formed a *tuath* or tribe, which gives the oldest territorial unit of old Ireland — about the size of a modern barony. Tribes were sometimes grouped in loose confederacies but no special word seems to have been usual for them. The plural of *tuath*, namely *tuatha*, seems to have served. All *tuatha* were not equal. Those of the earlier inhabitants of Ireland whom the Gaels defeated were held in various degrees of vassalage and must pay tribute to the conquerors.[10]

Thus while class divisions were appearing at the base of Irish society, the embryo of the territorial state was forming at the apex. The process took centuries. Class divisions were accentuated during the long prosperity coinciding with the "dark ages" of Europe, when slaves were imported from Britain to tend the growing cattle population.

A powerful force making for unification was Christianity with its universalist drive towards "one church and one king." The upheavals of the Danish wars tended in the same direction. The *tuath* was eliminated as a distinct territorial unit. Its constituent *clanna* were often dispersed in opposite directions. Similarly the septs of a *clann* were frequently scattered, and *clanna* were artificially reconstituted from unrelated septs. The result was to make of the Irish, so to speak, one tribe.

By the time the Normans came, the Irish undoubtedly possessed an all-Ireland consciousness of themselves as a people. But they were not yet a nation, but a loosely knit assemblage of confederated kinship groups.* Their qualities of democracy, solidarity and freedom from servility came into full play in self-defence. These were the qualities of the kinsmen. But the fatal weakness was the territorial limitation. The essential unit, the unit that mattered, was the largely self-sufficient group in a small area. This did not provide for the countrywide unity needed to defeat the invader. In sum, though a people, they were not yet a nation.

---

*P.S.O'Hegarty[11] would disagree. He saw as the enduring element in Ireland's long resistance the memory of the old kingship established by Niall Naoigiallach around 390 A.D. which survived till the invasions. But it never achieved the organisation of a territorial state and it is surely sounder to see the element of continuity in the common ownership of the sept land. This is what the kinsmen fought for.

THE INVADERS

Irish society was ripe for the transition to feudalism. Over the greater part of Britain it had already been established. This is the secret of the unending war that opened in the fatal year 1169.

It should be stated however, that it was not the English people, but their conquerors, who threw themselves on Ireland. The history of England shows this clearly. The Roman conquest of Britain destroyed the kinship system in the south and east while leaving it in the north and west, with the suckers of Roman taxation affixed to it in whatever degree was found practicable. It may thus not be merely the geographical fact that the English landed on the south and east coasts that explains why they took the old Romanised area easily enough while the north and west offered a long resistance.

Though it is disputed, their place names seem to indicate that the Anglo-Saxons re-established a kinship society in southern Britain, now England. But "even before they entered Britain their tribal organisation was rapidly disintegrating."[12] Certainly it possessed far less stability than that of the Irish, possibly from the rapid and recent acquisition of the new territories and the conversion of the Britons into an underprivileged class. The Liberal historian J.R. Green speaks of "an increasing degradation of the bulk of the people in the ninth century" and explains that "from Aelfred's day it was assumed that no man could exist without a lord"[13] Indeed he was enjoined to get himself one.[14] The lord of the soil became supreme and the day of the kinsmen was over. They no longer defended each other. Their lords defended them. The kingdom of all England was established by the Danes, after which a new conqueror, William the Norman, strengthened and systematised the feudal system to a degree not previously imagined, and established on English soil "an army which could only be maintained by a vast confiscation of the soil,"[13] which accordingly took place, further destroying the old democratic system.

FIRST PLANTATION

What the Normans later attempted in Ireland they performed first in England. In doing so they set in motion a chain of cause and effect which ultimately transferred the leadership of English democracy from the country to the town, and prepared the way for the overthrow of the feudal system in its own turn. Popular hatred of feudal oppression came out in repeated revolts of the impoverished and land-hungry peasantry,

21

of which the annals of England are full. Already by the time of William Rufus, what T.A. Jackson called the "unemployment problem peculiar to feudalism" had reared its head. What was to be done with the younger (and the illegitimate) sons of the nobility? Rufus carried out the first colonial experiment of the Anglo-Norman monarchy in his invasion of South Wales as far as Cardigan, and the first plantation, the plantation of Pembroke.[13] The result was to fan flames of resistance in Wales and, apart from the vicinity of the planted area, to disappoint grievously the fledging lords. Henry himself met a series of disastrous defeats at the hands of the Welsh clans, and it is recorded that on his return from Ireland in April 1172, a woman, seeing him about to mount a stone on which it was prophesied that an English king would slip and die, sprang forward and addressed the stone:- "Avenge us today, Llechlafor! Avenge the people of this land![15]

An early product of this process was the breed of Norman-Welsh barons whose "unemployment problem" (rendered more difficult by their failure to expand to the north) was in 1169 to be solved at the expense of the Irish people. Thus it was not the Welsh people who took part in the invasion of Ireland but their would-be conquerors.

THE INVASION

All the history books record how when the septs of Leinster decided to exercise their right of deposing the provincial king, Diarmait Mac Murchadha, who had needlessly involved them in a dispute with the O'Rourkes, Diarmait fled to the court of Henry of England and, swearing fealty to him as a vassal, asked his assistance in recovering his "rights." This was the first assertion of a feudal right to Irish soil, and two things need to be said, first that such would have arisen in some form or other as an inevitable result of the development of Irish society, and second that Henry did not need it as an inducement to instigate the plunder of Ireland. The feudal system in England was ready for the swallow; and Henry claimed to have held for some years past a bull of Pope Adrian assigning him Ireland as part of his dominions. The tragedy was not the institution of feudal property as such in Ireland, since this was inevitable, but the disastrous form this took, with the consequent retardation of Irish social, economic and political development.

The purpose of the invasion, begun by Strongbow and his companions, but followed up by Henry and his successors, was the reduction of Ireland to the status of a feof of the King of England.

RESISTANCE

The resistance of the Irish was so vigorous and unrelenting that it outlasted the feudal system in England. But it was not sufficiently united to drive out the invaders altogether. The result was a division of the country, not a definite permanent division, but a polarisation. Around Dublin, sometimes dominating the entire south-east, was the planted "pale," whose people for centuries spoke English and regarded themselves as English. Outside it, again varying in extent, was the Gaeltacht whose people spoke Irish and preserved kinship customs. A complex interaction developed in which the stronger effect was invariably the gaelicising of the conquerors.

The problem for the rulers of England was how, using the Pale as base, to bring about the submission of the Gaeltacht. As T.A. Jackson[7] described the situation:- "The Anglo-Norman lords, with their private armies, advanced across the great central plain . . . the Irish retreated with their cattle to the hills, the woods, and hiding places in the bog-country. On the level plains the clansmen stood no chance against the armoured Norman spearmen and their professional archers. In the hill country the reverse was the case, and every defile was a death trap. . . Thus as a first result the Normans got possession of large tracts of empty land; but in nearly every case the Irish, hidden in their lurking places, were only a night's march away, ready to pounce on cattle, barns or outlying parties." The difficulty of attracting English settlers under these conditions is obvious. Without colonists the only stable basis for operations was a compromise with the septs, permitting the old life to continue subject to the imposition of certain feudal tributes. Backsliding Normans who made such arrangements were sometimes impeached as traitors, but the economic advantage was so solidly with those who gained the sympathy of the Irish that by the time of the Statute of Kilkenny (1366) these were the majority and had grown "more Irish than the Irish themselves." They had many of them adopted Irish dress and customs, fitting themselves into the kinship system and ignoring alike exhortation from the Pale and the writ of the King of England.

The other side of this process was the increasing penetration of the old kinship society with feudal customs. The new chiefs were, and the old chiefs became in practice, fully hereditary. The *fuidhir* or unfree section, within the productive system but not of the kinship, lost the safeguards they had formerly enjoyed. The *clanna* had been dispersed again and except in the north-west the new chiefs had increased their power over the "somewhat fortuitous" recombinations of septs.[7] Yet as a result of the compromise, economic progress began again, wealth accumulated and huge fairs took place in the Gaeltacht whose commerce extended as far as the Mediterranean and the Baltic. During this period the English kings were distracted by internal difficulties in England. They therefore tolerated the feudalised Irish "middle nation" (typified by the Fitzgeralds) and failed to provoke Ireland to rebellion during the one period when such rebellion would almost certainly have been attended with success.

THE RISE OF THE WEST

In 1453 came the fall of Byzantium which finally blocked the land route to Asia and gave the stimulus to the great voyages of discovery which resulted in the invasion and colonisation of America. This was a great turning point in European history, since the apex of development was switched from the Mediterranean to the Atlantic seaboard. From that time on, ever accelerating in its urgency, arose a new English policy towards Ireland, that of assimilation. The aim was at all costs to prevent the establishment west of England of a rival as strong as Spain.

While the conditions for this change were maturing, English feudalism entered its final stage of absolute monarchy. It was Henry VIII who decided to break the truce with the "middle nation" and prevent those who had long ceased to be an effective agency for England becoming the representatives of Ireland. The method adopted was treachery followed by murder. Almost the entire senior branch of the Fitzgerald family was enticed to England and hanged at Tyburn.

The old system was then attacked at its weakest point. The chiefs were flattered with titles into becoming agencies of anglicization, in return for the personal ownership of the soil. If the clansmen submitted they became tenants, under various feudal tenures, good, bad or indifferent according to circumstances. If they refused, the chief was provided with a punitive expedition to quell them. If he did not avail himself of the offer he was himself attainted as a traitor.

Yet such was the resilience of the old society that a further compromise had to be come to. The right of the kinsman in the common land was so deeply ingrained that it was so to speak resurrected under the new conditions of tenancy. It became a claim to ownership within tenancy and in one of its forms became famous as the "Ulster custom."

24

It is widely held that this was brought to Ireland by Scottish settlers, as it was certainly preserved by the growth of the linen industry. But it is of native Irish growth.[16] It seems to have survived longest in Ulster because there the clans were longest preserved. Elsewhere it was lost and regained, lost and fought for again, under the title of the "good old modus" and its interest, theoretically speaking, is that an extinguished kinship right seems to have reappeared as a capitalist right, the claim by the tenant to a disposable goodwill in his tenancy, sometimes described as a "joint ownership."

At this point it is possible to assess the effect of the conquest. Partial and inconclusive though it was, it nevertheless transformed the Irish social system and contained kinship society in a kind of feudal box.

The question then arises, since feudalism was the more advanced system, did the conquest not make for progress, and did the Normans and their successors not do Ireland a good turn? The answer is that if Ireland had been left undisturbed Irish feudalism would have established itself quite early. It was the constant disturbance which made this impossible.

The happiest transition from tribal society to the territorial state was seen in Greece and Rome under the influence of their own internal needs. By introducing feudalism as a foreign system with which the Irish people were unable to identify themselves, the invaders preserved the attachment to the old forms, while forcibly smashing their organisation.

They compelled popular sentiment to look nostalgically to the golden age of the past; yet in doing so they laid the foundations of a modern peasantry which still preserved the gentile qualities of solidarity, democracy and aptitude for cooperation. These qualities moreover ceased to be local and contributed to the intense national and class solidarity the Irish people are capable of.

Putting the matter another way, until the sixteenth century Irish resistance was progressive as a struggle for the freedom of the Irish people to end kinship society in their own way, which was the most satisfactory, speedy and conclusive way for them. After that their aims passed ahead of their conquerors since they led to a new form of society which was beyond the invaders' scope. It should be noted too that the conflict between tenant right and landlord right within one tenure led across a long *via dolorosa* as Connolly called it, to the extinction of landlordism in favour of a peasant proprietary, which is itself now being threatened through the impact of imperialism. The descendant of the ancient clansman has become a small capitalist.

TUDOR PLANTATIONS

As the Atlantic opened up the attempts to assimilate Ireland grew more frantic. The first state experiment in large-scale clearance and plantation was made during the reign of Queen Mary. Failure to induce Englishmen to settle as planters led to the original clansmen returning to the planted area as tenants. The English would not accept as an opportunity what the Irish would only take as a necessity. After this failure in Leix-Offaly, in Elizabeth's time a substantial effort was made to plant Munster, in which the sycophant poet Edmund Spenser greatly enriched himself.

That gentleman wished to bring the Irish rebel "so low that he shall have no heart nor ability to endure his wretchedness . . . so pluck him on his knees that he will never be able to stand up again."[17]

Sir John Davies reported that the Irish "having been brayed, as it were in a mortar with sword, pestilence and famine, became altogether admirers of the Crowne of England."[18]

But lest the gilt should wear off the gingerbread, a proclamation from Sir Arthur Chichester explained that any relapse would be punished on "every one of them by all ways and means possible, to the utter extirpating and rooting out of them, their names and generations for ever."[19]

It was during the period of the Elizabethan atrocities that the potato, that could be stored by burial, replaced corn as the staple diet of the Irish peasant. But for the introduction of that vegetable Chichester's threats might have come into effect, for Irish resistance did not cease.[20]

REFORMATION

The opening up of the New World hastened changes which were already gathering within England. Wealth and commerce reached unprecedented development and began to press hard on the feudal laws which now restrained their further growth. England became a nation, and in the effort to create for it a unified consciousness, Shakespeare put on the stage practically the whole of English history from the reign of King John to that of Elizabeth.

With capitalism came the democracy of the towns and the Reformation, which was twofold in character. For the landlords it excused the expropriation of the estates of the church, which were then integrated into the growing mercantile system. For the capitalists it was a protection of their united national market against European feudalism. But some of the extreme Protestant sects reflected the interests of the small peasants and the rudimentary working class.

The attempt now made to impose the reformed religion on Ireland had as its object the cutting off of that country from possible allies on the Continent, and also the justification of further land-robbery to the British people who were becoming a power to be reckoned with once more. The effort of James I to plant Ulster was no more successful than those of Mary and Elizabeth. Land titles changed hands. The tillers of the soil had one more exaction piled above those they sustained already. But they remained. The aim of the plantation was not achieved. But the development of a new "middle nation" was more difficult under the new conditions. The English of the Pale and the most recent planters were Protestant. The tenantry remained Catholic. A further complication was the arrival of Scottish settlers in the Counties of Antrim and Down.[21] Those who arrived early in the century took lands cleared by the ravages of the arch-robber Chichester, those of the older inhabitants who remained having to withdraw to patchy ground on the hills where they huddled together on tiny holdings. A number of the settlers were artisans from Edinburgh and Glasgow, others peasants ruined by the enclosures of the common land which was proceeding in Scotland at this time.[22] It used to be said in Scotland of any alleged evil-doer that he would "end up in Ireland." In the middle years of the century came upwards of 50,000 families fleeing from religious persecution and bringing bitter memories of the treatment of Dissenters.[23] In dispossessing the native Irish they forged themselves fresh chains, and this contradiction in the position of the northern Dissenters should be borne in mind. Many of them suffered a needless second emigration as a consequence.[24]

ENGLISH REVOLUTION
The conquest of Ireland was completed only after the English revolution had destroyed the absolute monarchy and cleared the way for the development of capitalism . That struggle lasted some fifty years with fortunes of war which varied from time to time. Control of Ireland, important in relation to Continental enemies, was ten times more so in relation to civil war in England. Hence while making the progressive

claim to establish a bourgeois constitution in Britain, the English Parliament advanced simultaneously the reactionary claim to continue the overlordship of Ireland.

The year 1641 was marked by the first country-wide rising of the Irish people, reflecting the new unity forced on the feudalised clansmen. It was put down with the utmost ferocity and followed by a new and most extensive plantation, which caused more chaos but to no greater effect than the previous ones. The Irish tenantry could not be replaced. But the remnants of the gentile system were finally scattered by the sword of Cromwell in a war which cost the lives of two-fifths of the population of Ireland. In this era of blood and wickedness the Irish nation took final shape. But the whole of the eighteenth century was required to fill out the shape with reality.

THE LEVELLERS

At the close of the revolutionary period England entered the path of capitalist development unhindered by feudal obstacles, despite an antiquated political system which came up for change later. With the appearance of capitalism had come a rudimentary working class and even so soon the first declarations of solidarity with Ireland from the English people.

In 1641 Cromwell had worked up intense anti-Irish feeling for use against the King by alleging a "massacre of Protestants in Ireland" which did not take place."[7] In 1649 the "Leveller"* William Walwyn was imprisoned in the Tower for, among other things, asserting "that the sending over of Forces to Ireland is for nothing else but to make way by the blood of the army to enlarge their territories of power and Tyranny, that it is an unlawful War, a cruel and bloody work to go to destroy the Irish natives for their consciences."[25] Walwyn was prepared to take this stand although he actually believed that the Irish had massacred thousands of Protestants.

Walwyn is also believed to have written an attack on the Irish war entitled "The bloody project"[26] in which he asks the soldiers:-

---

*The Leveller ideology was greatly influenced by the teachings of the Anabaptists, one of the more extreme Dissenting sects. Here lies the germ of the alliance of Catholic and Dissenter in favour of toleration.

"Consider, as things now stand, to what end you should hazard your lives against the Irish. Will you go on still to kill, slay and murder in order to make them (your officers) as absolute lords and masters over Ireland as you have made them over England. Or is it your ambition to reduce the Irish to the happiness of tithes upon treble damages, or excise, customs and monopolies in trades? Or to fill their prisons with poor disabled persons, to fill their land with swarms of beggars . . . to take down monarchical tyranny and set up an aristocratical tyranny . . . Before you go, see those evils reformed here . . . And it would be much more to be wished that you might overcome them by just and equal offers than by strength and force."

About the same time the English Levellers issued manifestoes demanding complete liberty of conscience to include both Catholics and Dissenters. They also called for annual Parliaments, abolition of the Lords' veto, the ending of imprisonment for debt, abolition of tithes, security of tenure for small peasants, and the election of magistrates and militia officers.

This programme represents the true foundation of English democracy. Its origin shows moreover that the independence of Ireland was a demand of British democracy from its inception. Tradition was departed from whenever it was left out. The friends of Ireland then as now were to be found in the parties of most radical reform in England. And from the days of the Levellers to the present, however few they might be at any period, Ireland has never lacked champions among the English common people. It is worthy of note moreover that the first part of the eighteenth century when Ireland experienced her blackest days, was the time when English democracy found it most difficult to disentangle itself from the wreckage of past efforts and find a new way forward.

SUBJECTION

While it is true that the eighteenth century marks the deepest subjection of the Irish people, it is also true that from the commencement of this period time was on their side. Commerce and industry were developing and the interested classes in Britain were trying to hold them back. The struggle for the united home market had been joined, something impossible of achievement while the remnants of the tribal system survived. The new bourgeoisie was growing among the Protestants of the former Pale, the Catholics and the Ulster Dissenters. Only England's garrison, the large landlords, kept aloof from the processes of change while even they must take account of it. The necessities of the eighteenth century were gathered into a single sheaf by the impact of the American and French revolutions. The need of the day became the establishment of an independent Irish republic prepared to carry through an agrarian revolution and release Irish capitalism from all restraints on its development. The clearest sighted and most consistent exponent of this programme was Theobald Wolfe Tone. But before telling his story it will be necessary to examine the problems bequeathed him in somewhat greater detail.

2

Growth of a Nation

The opinion has sometimes been expressed by British writers, and among them unfortunately men whose views were otherwise strongly democratic, that the conquest of Ireland was justified by the "interests of the English revolution." This opinion is sown by the British ruling class. If true it would mean that the defeat of the English revolution was necessary in the interests of Irish independence. But in fact the placing of the interests of democracy in the two countries in this kind of opposition has done more to confuse opinion on the Irish question than any other misunderstanding.

The solution to the apparent antinomy was given historically in that brief flash when the old Irish democracy and the new English democracy met for a moment, saluted each other so to speak, and then parted for ever. The most progressive force in Ireland during the Cromwellian period was that of the Ulster clansmen led by Owen Roe O'Neill, Ireland's greatest leader before Tone.[27] His war aims included religious toleration and the restoration of the land to the Ulster clans. The latter could, of course, only have taken a new form. The most progressive in England, as has already been indicated, was that of the Levellers, represented for example by Walwyn, but also for a time by General Monk, who was credited with Leveller sympathies.

It was after driving the Scots from Derry that Owen Roe entered into negotiations with General Monk which could, if successful, conceivably have led to the establishment of an Irish Republic alongside and in alliance with the new English Republic, with the breaking of the power of the landed aristocracy in both countries, in sum a revolution nearer to that of 1789 in France.

This possibility was destroyed by the English Parliament which ordered Monk to break off the negotiations, and in August 1649, shortly before Owen Roe died, as was believed, at the hands of the poisoner,

Cromwell himself arrived in Dublin to pursue the alternative of reduclng Ireland to the status of a colony of the British Parliament.

There was of course even in English law no justification for this. The king was deposed. The London sovereignty died with him as Scotland showed by proclaiming Charles II king of Scotland. But the English Parliament relied on Poyning's Law, which made decisions of the Irish Parliament dependent on the English king's privy council. One might have thought "no king no council." But Cromwell knew well that "eleven men well armed will certainly subdue one man in his shirt."

The final destruction of the clans followed as automatically as the persecution of the Levellers. The result was that at the next crisis, that of 1688-91, neither British nor Irish democracy was able to act independently. The former clansmen now followed the Catholic landlords; the descendants of the Levellers, as Monmouth's rebellion showed, formed a radical faction within the Whig party. Though hailed in history books as the "Glorious Revolution" the deposition of James II and the installation of William of Orange merely restored the compromise which had ended the Cromwellian period. That compromise had been reached at the expense of the common people of the two countries. In 1688-91 this compromise was confirmed. The further issues of 1649 were not raised again. As a consequence the struggles of the two peoples followed separate paths until a long period of development brought them together again.

PATRIOT PARLIAMENT

When the "'Patriot Parliament" was called in Dublin by James in 1689, it declared the English Parliament incompetent to pass laws for Ireland; made the Irish House of Lords the final court of appeal in law cases, decreed complete religious toleration to be the law of Ireland (something demanded in England only by the Levellers) and enacted that tithes, though still compulsory for the tenant, should be paid by him to the church of his choice. None of these proposals could harm British democracy, nor could the revocation of the Cromwellian settlement, which would have weakened a landed aristocracy whose estates were scattered between the two countries.

On the other hand, the aristocratic nature of the Patriot Parliament was shown by its failure to alleviate in the slightest degree the dependent position of the tenantry. Moreover, as soon appeared, James's support for its proposals proved to be no more than demagogy, a fact which when it was realised, together with his cowardly behaviour, earned him the well known sobriquet, Séamus a' chaca. His aim was the re-conquest of England, after which his Irish allies could whistle for their freedom.

The balance of power on a European scale, as well as the undeveloped state of the democratic movement in the two countries, precluded the solution immediately visible that the two countries should separate with James retaining Ireland and William having England. In such circumstances James could have only temporarily held Ireland against its people. For that reason he must re-conquer Britain, an enterprise in which the mass of the Irish had not the slightest interest.''[28]

William for his part would have become dependent on the radical Whig (ex-Leveller) faction if he had failed to conquer Ireland — something his Whig supporters seem to have sensed when they proved so reluctant to provide him with an army for the Irish campaign.[7] Thus both sides had an interest in fighting the war to a finish. It was the common interest of the landed aristocracy. The common people ''fought not their enemies but the enemies of their enemies.'' If the historians of the ''good old cause'' claim that William's victory (over which *Te deums* were sung in Rome) was the most progressive possible outcome, the modern British worker should reflect that it placed the British landlord classes in a position which proved almost unassailable for two centuries, and which is far too strong today.

BREACH OF FAITH

William won the war and the ''articles of capitulation'' were signed in Limerick on October 13th 1691. This was the so-called ''Treaty of Limerick''. Not for the last time were ''articles of agreement'' dignified with the title of ''Treaty'' to win Irish faith and graded down again when English faith was to be broken.

''The whole history of Ireland, from that day until the year 1793, consists of one long and continual breach of the treaty.'' So said John Mitchel.[29] Attempts have been made to shuffle responsibility on to the Irish. But there is no doubt whatsoever that the treachery was the responsibility of the English Government.

What William agreed at Limerick was as follows:- ''The Roman Catholics of this kingdom shall enjoy such privileges in the exercise of their religion as are consistent with the laws of Ireland; or as they did enjoy in the reign of King Charles the Second . . . and their majesties, as soon as their affairs will permit them to summon a Parliament in this kingdom, will endeavour to procure the said Roman Catholics such further security as may preserve them from any disturbance upon the account of their said religion." In other words, the *status quo ante* was to be returned to pending measures of Catholic relief. That status quo involved certain penal laws, but did not involve provisions barring Catholics from Parliament

The articles of Limerick were breached just two months after they were signed and by the English Parliament. A Bill was sent to the Lords providing that no person should sit in the Irish Parliament, nor hold any Irish office, civil, military or ecclesiastical, nor should practise law or medicine in Ireland until he had taken the oaths of allegiance and supremacy, and subscribed a declaration against transubstantiation. The Bill became law and received the Royal Assent. When next year Catholic peers and commons presented themselves at the Parliament in Dublin they were excluded thanks to the English Act.

Encouraged by their English masters, the Dublin Parliament then adopted another English Act which imposed confiscation upon all Irish landowners who had taken part with James. After an appeal to William the matter was settled by the Catholics surrendering three-quarters of a million acres of land.

The English Government possessed complete sovereignty in Ireland. It established a Parliament handpicked for its servility and urged it into collision with the majority of the Irish people. It then stood back, leaving its creatures to incur the odium, confining itself to occasional adroit interventions designed to maintain the dissensions it had started. Sometimes when persecution flagged it encouraged it. At other times it put on a spurious show of surprise at the result of its own handiwork.

PENAL LAWS

A process now began which within the space of a few years reduced the Catholics of Ireland to something approaching the conditions of Africans under apartheid. The royal speech of August 27th 1695, by the mouth of the king's deputy, indicated the policy required of the Irish Parliament. They were recommended:-

"to lay hold of the opportunity then put into their hands of making such a lasting settlement that it might never more be in the power of their enemies to put England to expense of blood and treasure." The monstrous hypocrisy of this statement is apparent when one reflects that "England" could have

*saved all her blood and treasure by the simple expedient of minding her
own business and keeping her troops at home, as the English Levellers
had proposed.*

The Dublin Parliament, whose members, it should be remembered,
regarded themselves as English, that is to say as a colony like that of
New England, went to work with a will. They introduced substantial
modifications into the articles of Limerick, to which they had not been
a party, all to the disadvantage of the Catholics. They deprived
"papists" of the right to bear arms, or undertake the education of their
own children. They banished "all the regulars of the popish clergy."
In 1696 they forbade Catholics to act as solicitors or gamekeepers.

In 1704 an Act to "prevent the further growth of Popery" restrained
a Catholic father from disposing of his estate if his son were a Protestant,
depriving him of the custody of his own child, of whatever age, should
he profess himself a Protestant, incapacitated a Catholic son from
inheriting from a Protestant father, and prohibited Catholics from buying,
or even renting ground for more than thirty-one years.[30] In 1707 it
was provided that a convert might file a Bill in Chancery to reduce his
Catholic father's estate in fee simple to a life-tenancy, with remainder
in fee to the son. A pension of £30 was offered to converted priests
and rewards offered for the "better discovery of recusant Popish
clergymen and schoolmasters" on a sliding scale starting at £10 for
an usher and £50 for an archbishop.

In 1708 Catholics were debarred from serving on grand juries. A
militia Bill provided for the seizure of their horses, taxing them double
for the cost of the militia, and excluding them from constabulary and
nightwatch duties, with liability to pay handsomely for Protestant
substitutes. In 1723 the Dublin Parliament went to the fantastic length
of passing a Bill which provided for the castration of Catholic priests.
This was forwarded to London and only rejected as a result of the
intervention of the French premier Cardinal Fleury.[30] Needless to say
a code so draconic could not be put into full effect and there was
widespread evasion.

Four years later at the accession of George II the Irish Catholics
endeavoured to ingratiate themselves with the new monarch by
presenting a loyal address which was never forwarded to him. They
were requited by losing the parliamentary franchise, which they could
in any case only exercise in favour of their enemies, and remained totally

disfranchised for 67 years. The position to which the Catholics of Ireland were ultimately reduced is summarised by a judgement given in the Four Courts in 1759 in the case of O'Toole, that "the law did not presume a Papist to exist in the kingdom, nor could they breathe without the connivance of the Government."

During this period the landlord class undertook the most wasteful clearance of Irish timber and began the enclosure of the common lands. For two generations the people were too cowed to offer any effective resistance. The result was seen in two famines, one in 1728 and another in 1741, the plight of the Irish tenant being such as was described in Swift's *Modest Proposal*.

RESTRAINTS ON TRADE

The one field in which Catholic enterprise was not debarred, save only emigration, was trade and industry. Here Britain used her supremacy in economic matters to preserve simultaneously the interests of her own manufacturers and those of the landlords in Ireland. When in 1703 the Irish lords suggested a union such as was imposed on Scotland in 1707 the English Parliament rejected it. A part reason was that the countries must be swallowed one at a time. For the rest a union would facilitate the access of Irish goods to the British and colonial markets, and the growth of an Irish bourgeoisie which might threaten the landlord supremacy.

An account of the restraints on Irish trade was presented to the Parliament by Hely-Hutchinson[31] at the end of the century. A useful summary from the pen of Lord Dufferin is given in S.G.Hobson's *Irish Home Rule:*-[32]

> "*One by one, each of our nascent industries was either strangled in its birth or handed over, gagged and bound, to the jealous custody of the rival interest of England, until at last every fountain of wealth was hermetically sealed, and even the traditions of commercial enterprise have perished through desuetude. The owners of England's pastures had the honour of opening the campaign.*
>
> "*As early as the commencement of the eighteenth century the beeves of Roscommon, Tipperary and Queen's County undersold the produce of the English grass counties in their own market. By*

36

an Act of Parliament cattle were declared 'a nuisance' and their importation prohibited. Forbidden to send our beasts alive across the channel, we killed them at home and began to supply the sister country with cured provisions. A second Act of Parliament imposed prohibitory duties on salted meats. The hides of the animals still remained; but the same influence put a stop to the importation of leather. Our cattle trade abolished, we tried sheep farming. The sheep-breeders of England immediately took alarm, and Irish wool was declared contraband.

"Headed off in this direction, we tried to work up the raw material at home; but this created the greatest outcry of all. Every maker of fustian, flannel and broadcloth in the country rose up in arms and by an Act of William III the woolen industry of Ireland was extinguished and 20,000 manufacturers left the island. The easiness of the Irish Labour market and the cheapness of provisions still giving us an advantage even though we had to import our materials, we next made a dash at the silk business; but the English silk manufacturer, the sugar refiner, the soap and candle maker (who specially dreaded the abundance of our kelp) and every other trade or interest that thought it worth its while to petition, was received by Parliament with the same partial cordiality, until the most searching scouting failed to detect a single vent through which it was possible for the hated industry of Ireland to respire.

"But although excluded from the markets of England, a hundred harbours gave her access to the universal sea. Alas, a rival commerce on her own element was still less welcome to England, and as early as the reign of Charles II the Levant, the ports of Europe, the oceans beyond the Cape of Good Hope were forbidden the flag of Ireland.

"The colonial trade alone was in a manner open, if that can be called an open trade which for a long time precluded all exports whatever, and excluded from direct importation to Ireland of such important articles as sugar, cotton and tobacco.

"What has been the consequence of such a system, pursued with relentless pertinacity for two hundred and fifty years? This — that, debarred from every other trade and industry, the entire nation flung itself back upon the land with as fatal an impulse as when a river, whose current is suddenly impeded, rolls back and drowns the valley it once fertilised."

37

THE NORTH

That British policy was aimed at maintaining the exploitation of Ireland as a feudal estate, and discouraging bourgeois development, both economic and political, is illustrated by the experience of the northern Dissenters. The establishment of the linen industry in Lisburn at the end of the seventeenth century was followed by a rapid development affecting all sides of its manufacture from flax-growing to sun-bleaching of the brown pieces. Ancillary industries slowly established themselves in the Lagan valley and the rising prosperity of this mainly Protestant area would, on any purely sectarian argument, have been expected to delight the anti-Catholic Govermment. Instead, the policy inaugurated from England was to prevent the northern bourgeoisie from securing any influence in civil affairs.

Accordingly, when a Bill from the Irish Parliament was considered in London in 1704 , the English House of Commons deliberately inserted in it a clause compelling Dissenters to take a "sacramental test" before being admitted into public office. When the result was virtually to wipe out the corporation of Belfast, encouraged by its masters, the Dublin Parliament took powers to appoint substitutes from the established church. This proved easier said than done and once more the full force of the law was evaded.

Because it stood alone in opposition to Catholicism in Scotland, Presbyterianism could not be subjected to the type of penalty inflicted on the Catholics. The result was that the Dissenters kept up a continuous agitation against the Test Act throughout the century. At first they acquiesced in the supposed common interest of Protestantism against Catholicism. Perhaps Dean Swift helped to clear their minds. That "bad subject but worse rebel," as Daniel O'Connell called him, issued a *reductio ad absurdum* of the Presbyterian claim to toleration which pointed out that every argument they used could be used with equal force in favour of the Catholics. From then on their fanaticism against "popery" tended to decline.

Ulster, where the clans had survived longest, where the tenant preserved some vestige of his ancient rights, and where capitalism was most rapidly developing together with an industrial working class, was the first and sharpest force of the Irish people against the eighteenth century ascendancy.

PATRIOT PARTY

But the ruthlessness of British commercial policy was such that it corresponded to the interests only of the largest, most recently established or irrevocably absentee landlords. At point after point it came into collision with those who had bourgeois interests and connections, and with the Protestant merchants and manufacturers of the towns. Consequently there grew up a "patriot" literature from which protests on minor issues advanced to the position of claiming for the English colony in Ireland the rights of a nation. More slowly, and with less immediate effect, there emerged within the Irish Parliament a "patriot party". The literature was first associated with the names of Molyneux and Swift, who pronounced themselves Englishmen, later with that of Bishop Berkeley, who called himself an Irishman, and denounced the horrors of the famines.

The first parliamentary skirmish took place in 1719 when the British House of Lords set aside a judgement of the Irish peers. The dispute was terminated by a "Declaratory Act" of the British Parliament to the effect that the Lords and Commons of Great Britain could legislate for Ireland, and that the Irish House of Lords had no legal powers whatever. Not until the year 1741 did a vigorous and permanent opposition develop. Its initiator was Dr. Lucas, a fanatical anti-papist but a man of great energy and character, imbued with the strange half-nationalism of the colony, and determined to put Swift's precepts into effect. In the process he won the support of the Dublin middle and working classes, and in the third quarter of the century, Dublin displayed its strong "Lucassian" persuasions in "many a ruction." In 1751 and 1753 there were tussles with the British Parliament over the right to dispose of surplus revenue.

The Irish Parliament was now brought to heel by means of bribery, and from then on shameless corruption was added to the jewels the administration was already wearing in its crown. But Britain had a second rod in pickle. That was a project for a legislative union between the two countries which was to be put into effect should the Irish Parliament prove completely intractable. It was intended to achieve this through the Catholics, making use of the disgust the Irish administration had aroused through its obedience to those who were now getting ready to submerge it.

CATHOLIC AGITATION

It was against this background that the Catholics themselves began to revive the agitation for toleration. Following the O'Toole judgement, a number of prominent Catholics including Dr. Curry, author of *Historical Review of the Irish Wars*, established the Catholic Committee. Its immediate purpose was to complete the legal recognition of the existence of Catholics.

This modest aim was accomplished by the presentation of a loyal address to the House of Hanover at a time when the Seven Years War looked like going badly for England. The address was most graciously received and acknowledged in Britain, but not at first in Ireland. Ultimately, however, it was read in the House of Commons by Speaker MacDermott, and the Catholics were accorded official recognition for the first time since the articles of Limerick. Simultaneously with the new-found courage of the middle-class Catholics came a wave of agrarian discontent culminating in what T.A. Jackson[7] called the "first-recorded general uprising of the peasantry" in 1761. British economic policy had led to impossible conditions in the countryside and an acute agrarian crisis was precipitated by the abnormal conditions of the Seven Years War. The peasantry carried on their backs a pyramid of middlemen with the great landlord at the apex. The increased demand for agricultural products encouraged landlords to carry out evictions in favour of grass-farming. The practice grew of putting up tenancies to auction.

The last straw was the carrying out by the landlords of large-scale enclosures of the remaining common land, which began in Co. Limerick and spread throughout Munster. In Waterford, Cork and Tipperary angry crowds tore down the enclosures (whence as in England the name "Levellers") and soon the south was aflame with the "Whiteboy" disturbances. Scarcely had these been suppressed and their supposed leaders hanged than the "Oakboys" appeared in Co. Monaghan where the movement spread into Co. Tyrone and Armagh.

The Ulster agrarian societies were composed entirely of Protestants, and not only put up a resistance to fines for the renewal of tenancies, rack-rents, tithes and attempts to introduce grass farming, but also began to organise rural industrial workers to resist their employers. So began the first independent actions of the Irish working-class, which steadily increased in power and importance, even though in 1764 a clear-cut victory was out of the question. The identity of interest between the Protestant and Catholic tenantries further encouraged the middle-class Catholics, and impressed the need for a national movement.

40

CHALLENGES

Three-quarters of a century after the articles of Limerick had imposed on Ireland what seemed likely to be an endless servitude, the settlement was being challenged on all sides, from the Dissenting bourgeoisie and the workers of the north, from the Protestant merchants, traders and artisans of Dublin, from the Catholic middle-class of the south, from the rack-rented peasantry of all Ireland. And confronted by this situation the large and small landowners of the Ascendancy had divided into a loyal and a "patriot" party both of which required the constant injection of bribes to sweeten them to the requirements of their British masters. As the only "free" opposition the initiative belonged to the "Patriot" party but, as John Mitchel observed:-

> "The fatal weakness of the colony was that it could not amalgamate with the mass of the Irish people so as to form a true nation, but set up the vain pretence to hold down a whole disfranchised people with one hand, and defy England with the oth ."[29]

AMERICA

The event which led to the temporary victory of the "patriot" party in the colony, and a struggle against the commercial stranglehold of Britain, was the American revolution. The spearhead consisted of the northern Dissenters who won an alliance with the "patriot" middle class and small landowners of the established church. Before the latter withdrew in confusion from the leadership of the social forces they had set in motion, a fiscal and constitutional revolution had been accomplished.

No sooner had matters settled down to an uneasy compromise than the "lower orders," prepared by the example of their "betters," were stimulated by the French revolution to make their own trial of strength. In the result the British authorities waded through the blood of the Irish people to impose a fresh counter-revolutionary settlement. The Act of Union abolished the colonial Parliament, but it left the mass of the Irish people conscious of themselves once more as a nation, directly confronting the imperial power. It also drove the landlord class out of the ranks of the nation. The details of the process by which this effect came about are therefore of great interest and great importance.

The American revolution was occasioned by causes which the "patriot" party in Dublin immediately recognised, namely the

41

"mercantilist" policy of the British Government which aimed at the monopolising of colonial trade, the limitation of American industry by law, and for these purposes the maintenance of British supremacy. Throughout the period preceding the Declaration of Independence of 1776 the colonies had experienced navigation Acts, "molasses" Acts, "Stamp Acts" aimed at establishing the principle of taxation without representation, and a "Declaratory" Act exactly parallel with that reserving the right to legislate for Ireland. Nor was the weapon of religious sectarianism neglected. The strongly dissenting New Englanders were shocked when the British Government established Roman Catholicism as the religion of the province of Quebec, the purpose (apart from territorial considerations) being to create a balance in America as had been done in Ireland.

But the American colonies were far better placed than Ireland to resist Britain when, at the close of the Seven Years War, she imagined herself free from European commitments, and strove to enforce what had for some time past proved unenforceable. The colonies were thousands of miles away. Their coastline was too lengthy to be effectively patrolled. Their territory was too vast to be policed. And their population was being continually reinforced by immigrants who had no reason to love the class of merciless but astute robbers who ruled in London. From 1772 onward a network of "Corresponding Societies" radiated from Boston. Partial struggles on minor issues showed up the importance as well as the stupidity of the Government, encouraged the timid, exposed the treacherous, and finally led to the establishment of a colonial nation confronting on the one hand a distant executive, and on the other a weak disunited aboriginal population. When Britain tried to restore her position by force her European enemies joined with the Americans, helping at first by subsidies, later by war as well.

By 1778, Britain was hard pressed. Ireland was almost denuded of troops. French privateers were preying on British shipping, and fearing a repetition of the fate of Carrickfergus during the Seven Years War, the citizens of Belfast sent to Dublin Castle a request for a military force to protect their thriving industrial town. It was this demand which revealed the impotence of the executive which could do no more than urge Belfast to undertake its own defence. To do so was of course to invite revolution. A State without force is no State at all.

The citizens of Belfast within a short time raised several regiments of Volunteers, uniformed, armed and equipped by public subscription.

The movement spread throughout the country. The Government, thus already taken prisoner, could do no more than seek to divide the Volunteers (composed of both members of the Established Church and Dissenters) by sounding the alarm that arms might get into the hands of the Catholics. The Catholic bourgeoisie showed great political percipience in refraining from volunteering (with a few justifiable exceptions) but supporting the Volunteers financially.

THE VOLUNTEERS

Led by Belfast the people availed themselves of the opportunity to make themselves a military power in the land. The "patriot" party at once recognised in this situation the means of throwing off British commercial restraints, while keeping the revolution within the bounds of their class interests. They were assisted by the fact that the American revolution had fanned the smouldering fire of discontent in England. The anti-democratic character of the war, together with its dislocation of trade, was widely understood in Britain and while the Whigs, representing the forces of the industrial revolution, were also opposed to the war, there crystallised out a radical opinion soon to separate itself from the Whigs and so give birth to the dynasty of radical and democratic movements which has survived from that day to this. When the young Dublin barrister Henry Grattan in October 1779 rose in the Parliament to demand freedom of trade the objections of the most loyal, as of the most timid, were brushed aside and his vote was unanimous.

Faced with such a demand, backed by popular demonstrations in which the armed Volunteers played a notable part, the Government gave in. In December 1779 and January 1780 Acts of the British Parliament abolished nearly all the restraints on Irish trade. In April 1780 Grattan moved a resolution denying the right of the English Parliament to legislate for Ireland. The administration contrived to evade a vote and for two years a game of temporising and manoeuvring was played by the British authorities.

Their difficulty can be appreciated when one asks the question: "What power would bind Ireland to Britain once the British Parliament relinquished its legislative overlordship?" "The Crown?" Important only as implying executive functions which were effectively counterbalanced by the existence of the Volunteers. The system of official corruption? A prosperous Ireland would be independent of it. The common interest of the two nations? At this stage, as always, it

43

lay in separation plus co-operation. Clearly the only effective link was the need of the colony to be protected from the mass of the Irish people.

To remove this link was needed first the repeal of the penal laws, and second a parliamentary reform which would enfranchise the mass of the people. Without these measures Britain could still keep the nation divided and throw the revolution back again to its starting point .

The "patriot" party were prepared to move towards Catholic relief, but did so hesitantly. Their Catholic Relief Bill repealed the ordinances which debarred Catholics from bequeathing, inheriting or purchasing estates and for taking leases of 999 years. That is to say, the wealthier Catholics to whom the Whigs were bound by a sense of class solidarity were relieved.

The great Dungannon Convention of the Volunteers which met on February 15th 1782 reaffirmed the demand for legislative independence, denounced Poyning's law, and commended the "relaxation of the penal laws against our Roman Catholic fellow subjects." Strengthened by the clear mandate of the people, Grattan moved his Declaration of Irish Right in the same month, and the same British Government, with the Whigs now in power, gave in, conceding all Grattan's demands.[7] The Declaratory Act of 1719 was repealed in London, after which Poyning's Law (an Act of the Irish Parliament) was repealed in Dublin. Formal independence was thus established; but its contents depended entirely on the situation of freedom or slavery of the common people.

SIDETRACKED

It was at this point that the national movement was sidetracked by Flood's proposal to press the British Parliament for an express renunciation of the right to legislate for Ireland. The Ulster Volunteer Association met at Dungannon on September 8th. It was proposed to demand that the elective franchise should be restored to the Catholics. But through the agency of Lord Charlemont and his friends the motion was lost. The excitement of pursuing the "renunciation" hare diverted attention from the fact that the revolutionaries had baulked at their next task.

The machinery of bribery was now given full power by the Castle clique, while the British Parliament passed the Renunciation Act with scarce a thought. The minds of Britain's rulers were at ease for the moment. It is all but certain that from this time the British ruling class became converted to the necessity of a union. Playing about with

44

renunciations was quite subsidiary to their main strategy.

When the Grand National Convention of the Volunteers met in Dublin in November 1783, despite the fine talk, the enthusiasm, and the demands on the Government, once more despite the eloquent urging of the Belfast delegation, Catholic emancipation was rejected. The Government knew then that if the demands for moderate reform which the Volunteers were proposing were rejected, there was no fear of their undertaking the one activity that could enforce them, namely a common struggle with the Catholics. Amid demands from the administration for the "restoration of the sword to the executive" by the embodiment of militia, the indecisive men of the colony slunk away shamefacedly and earned the bitter taunts of the young Trinity College graduate, Theobold Wolfe Tone, who watched the performance without at that time understanding what it was about.

UNFINISHED REVOLUTION

During the ensuing years the British Prime Minister Pitt further extended the system of bribery, and began to insinuate what Grattan called "a creeping or incipient Union" beginning with the harmonisation of the navigation laws of the two countries. By this means the Irish Parliament was to be made a "mere registration office for British Acts." The proposals were withdrawn and Pitt had to bide his time. The Irish administration had accepted responsibility for the continuing misery of the common people by declining to remove the British-created system of oppression when it had the power to do so. It had placed itself in a position where it could go neither backward nor forward. Corruption flourished as never before, and the main result of the revolution of 1782 seemed to be that the value of every pocket borough in Ireland had doubled. As Wolfe Tone put it nine years afterwards:-

> *"The revolution of 1782 was a Revolution which enabled Irishmen to sell at a much higher price their honour, their integrity and the interests of their country; it was a revolution which while at one stroke it doubled the value of every borough-monger in the kingdom left three-fourths of our countrymen slaves as it found them, and the government of Ireland in the base and wicked, and contemptible hands who had spent their lives in degrading and plundering her . . . the power remained in the hands of our enemies, again to be exerted for our ruin, with this difference that formerly we had our*

distresses, our injuries, and our insults gratis at the hands of England; but now we pay very dearly to receive the same with aggravation, through the hands of Irishmen.'[33]

In such a situation Pitt's plan of a "creeping Union" might conceivably have proved successful. The gains of Grattan's revolution (more real than would appear from the biting words of Tone, who was concerned to take the people a further step forward) were being left to rust through misuse. But history came forward with a rare favour, a second opportunity within one decade. That was the French revolution of 1789. And the central figure in the struggle which ensued was Theobald Wolfe Tone, whose programme for Catholic emancipation, complete and unreserved, a democratic franchise putting the power into the hands of the Irish people, and finally an agrarian revolution, has been described as the "application of the rights of man to Ireland" and was certainly the first assertion of the principle of an Irish Republic.

3

Making of a Separatist

There have been many biographies of Wolfe Tone, the most famous being the "Life"[34] or autobiography edited by his son in 1826 and republished in abridged form by Barry O'Brien in 1893.[35] As Brian O'Higgins remarked,[36] this consists mainly of entries in a journal intended for the subsequent amusement of his wife, family and intimate friend Thomas Russell, and by light-hearted overstatement of quirks and foibles Tone unwittingly provided ammunition the enemies of his principles were only too ready to fire.

He has been equally disserviced by such undiscriminating admirers as Aodh de Blacam whose strained attempts to paint him as all but a practising Catholic need raise only a smile. Mr Denis Ireland's *Patriot Adventurer*[38] is workmanlike if not deeply penetrating. An excellent summary was Alice Milligan's long-forgotten biography written for the '98 Centenary celebrations at the end of the last century.[39]

The most serious study so far undertaken is that of Mr Frank MacDermot[40] who made a real effort to get at primary sources, but whose frankly declared lack of sympathy with Tone's "most cherished ideas," namely the excellence of the French revolution and the "iniquity of English influence in Ireland," led him into what most republicans will consider warped judgements of Tone's motives. In particular he seems to lay an undue emphasis on youthful pranks and foibles which have little significance in a life's work.

In general, Tone's biographers have neglected an important principle. It is as if in the political and intellectual, as well as the biological life of man, there is a kind of recapitulation. An embryo in course of development takes on the form of a fish, later a reptile, then a mammal and only after birth acquires the full mental characteristics of a man. Similarly an individual can appear to follow out through his youth stages of political development already undergone by his class. He achieves greatness in larger or smaller measure when, finally established as himself, he takes that development further along its necessary path. It is from this point of view that Tone's early life and development can best be judged.

He was born in "Lucassian" Dublin on 20th June 1763 at 44 Stafford Street, then a respectable district just past its prime. His father, Peter Tone, was a coach builder of farming stock in the prosperous corn-country of Kildare, and a member of the established church. The father's family had been Cromwellian planters, having freehold tenancies on the estate of the Wolfes of Blackhall, near Clane.

Peter's wife, Margaret, was the daughter of a sea captain named Lamport in Drogheda whom he seems to have met thanks to her connection with the Wolfe family. The eldest son of Peter and Margaret Tone was named Theobald Wolfe after a member of the family, whose son was to write the famous poem the *Burial of Sir John Moore*.

Whereas the parents were "pretty much like other people," the children were, according to their eldest brother, all possessed of a "wild spirit of adventure." The parents were farming people not really adjusted to the urban life of Dublin, and no doubt this expressed itself in the children. Theobald was sent to a good preparatory school and so impressed his teacher that he urged his father to send him to a Latin school in preparation for Trinity College where he might possibly achieve a fellowship.

The clergyman under whose charge he was next placed was able but careless. Peter had failed in business. He settled at Bodenstown, Co. Kildare, until a piece of family litigation in 1789 ruined him once more and drove him back to work under the Paving Board. Inadequately supervised, Theobald neglected his studies and spent his time walking in the country, bathing in the sea and watching parades of troops in the Phoenix Park. It was at this time he acquired an "untameable desire" to become a soldier. His father learned of his new passion, but refused to permit him to enter the Army. Returning to his studies with bad grace, he recovered lost time so successfully that he was able to enter Trinity College in February 1781.

CLASS BACKGROUND
Tone belonged to the small Protestant bourgeois class of Dublin, which was not directly concerned in the exploitation of the Catholics, but provided goods and services for the Ascendancy. This class was faced

with dangers and compensating opportunities. Within its dependence on the Ascendancy its main concern was lest English products should supplant its own in supplying the needs of Dublin. It had not shaken off the anti-Catholic jealousy of the privileged farmers of the Pale who provisioned Dublin; but its future depended on the political struggle for the defence of the national economy.

Tone's opinions at this period corresponded exactly to what would be expected from his social station. The British Army glittered with personal opportunity. The Americans were rebels. In the Trinity College historical society, of which he became auditor, his views were moderately conservative. He supported octennial as against triennial Parliaments, upheld the property qualification and the minimum age limit of thirty for members. He argued that the discovery of America was a misfortune for Europe.[40] But his class interests show clearly in two other things. He was opposed to imprisonment for debt, and he was a member of a committee of students who following the example of the non-importation leagues pledged themselves for the space of one year to buy only Irish manufactures.

All his contemporaries agree that he was a man of remarkable intellectual endowments. But it is clear that neither within the contradictory outlook of his own class, nor in that of the more privileged community he joined at Trinity College, was there adequate scope for them. His studies were consequently fitful. He underwent a temporary passion for the stage. At another time he immersed himself in military manuals. At the same time he kept up a series of love-affairs which culminated with his elopement with Matilda Witherington who became his wife at the age of fifteen.

She was the daughter of a draper, and while possessing expectations of an inheritance, belonged to the same social level as himself. Perhaps this is the secret of their happiness. There was much to disturb it. But they seem seldom to have exchanged a cross word.

COLLEGE AND LAW

The marriage took place in July 1785 and the bride's family seemingly deciding to accept what could not be cured, there was a reconciliation. Later there was a fresh breach and the couple went to live in Bodenstown. Tone secured his B.A. degree in February 1786, and since in order to become a barrister it was necessary to spend two years keeping terms in London, he left Ireland early in 1787.

Here he seems to have frittered away his time as before. Everything interested him but the drudgery of law. He contributed reviews to literary papers, collaborated in writing a novel, and prepared a scheme for the settlement of the Sandwich Islands which he submitted to William Pitt. Its rejection caused him intense chagrin.

That he should propose what today would be called an imperialist scheme should occasion no surprise. The class he belonged to in no way separated itself from Britain's colonial policy; and not till the rise of the Jacobins in France several years later was the doctrine of national self-determination even formulated. It could hardly be expected to sweep a Europe whose trade had fattened on the robbery of four continents. The absence from his mind of any over-riding purpose is illustrated by his account (over-written in the character of an exaggerated family joke) of his decision to join the service of the East India Company and "quit Europe for ever," and his unsuccessful attempt to do so. This would, of course, have involved abandoning his career, which though uninteresting to him, had its compensations, and deserting his wife and family. Madden[41] takes the story literally and allows Tone some vestige of an excuse, certainly not a justification. MacDermot[40] likewise accepts the story but disallows Madden's excuse. But it is Brian O'Higgins's warning that should be borne in mind. The memoirs were written for people who would know the full facts, and indeed share private jokes with him; if the full story consisted of the "treachery" MacDermott asserts, it is unlikely Tone would have adverted to it or his son published it.

At the end of 1788 Tone returned to Dublin, on his own admission "knowing no more of law than he did of necromancy." But faced with the necessity of equipping himself to earn a living, he borrowed £500 from Matilda's grandfather, bought £100 worth of law books and settled down to learn what he should have learned before.

He took his degree in Law in February 1789 and was called to the Bar soon afterwards. As a barrister he went the Leinster circuit three times, but found the practice of law as distasteful as its study had been, his lack of outstanding success being due also to a disinclination to "treat messieurs the attorneys, and to make them drink, a sacrifice of their respectability which even the most liberal minded of the profession are obliged to make." It was at this time his mind turned in the direction of politics.

POLITICS

The patriot party had been battering at the end of a political cul-de-sac since Charlemont had led and Flood covered the retreat from a democratic revolution. It was concerned with the incidentals rather than the basis of the uneasy compromise of 1783. A Whig club, established in Dublin around 1789, made it a standing order to "exclude all discussion of the Catholic question," and the famous Whig toast, "the Sovereignty of the people" was interpreted as excluding five Irishmen out of six. Its members included the Duke of Leinster, the Earl of Charlemont, together with Messrs. Connolly, Forbes, Ponsonby and Grattan. The only member of firm democratic views was the famous "people's advocate," John Philpot Curran.

The insanity of George III raised the issue of the right of the Irish Parliament to offer his son the regency apart from any such action on the part of the British Parliament. The problem was solved by the King's recovery, but both Pitt and his coadjutor in Ireland, Mr Fitzgibbon, "drew from it an argument for the total annihilation of Ireland by a legislative Union." And in the various debates on the subject of corruption the threat of the Union was repeatedly held over the heads of the patriot party.

A general election was held in April 1790, in preparation for which Tone, who now described himself as an "independent Whig", wrote his first political pamphlet.[34] It was such as might have come from the pen of any member of the "patriot party" possessed of Tone's sharp wit and capacity for suave invective.

The *Review of the conduct of the administration during the seventh session of Parliament* accused the administration of a "wanton profligacy" in the disposal of public money. Corruption had reached such a pitch that the Irish pensions list amounted to £108,280 annually (a greater sum than its English counterpart), £30,000 of which had been granted or re-granted since 1784. The Minister's majority of 144 included no less than 104 who were in enjoyment of public offices. If the "Place bill" proposed by the "patriot party" had been passed it would have been reduced to 52.

Tone roundly condemned the practice of selling peerages and applying the proceeds to purchasing seats in the Commons. He defended the right of printers to publish controversial material without being held to bail against possible libel in vexatious sums. In his dedication to the *Free people of Ireland* Tone makes an enthusiastic reference to the

51

Volunteers which possibly earned the suspicion of the Dublin Whigs, for they failed to elect him a member:-

> *"It is with some pride," he wrote, "that I find the mode proposed in the following pages has been anticipated by the inhabitants of Belfast; a city renowned over the kingdom and over England, for its thorough knowledge of and ardent attachment to constitutional liberty. I am a young man, but I remember the era when, from that very city, the torrent of public spirit rushed forth, overspread the land, and swept the ancient bulwarks of English tyranny before it."*[34]

Tone had thus reached an identity of opinion with the most advanced representatives of his class, the Dissenters of Belfast, and from that time on he went forward with the vanguard. The Northern Whigs reprinted his pamphlet and circulated it in large numbers, later discovering the identity of the author and making him an honorary member of their society.

NEUTRALITY

In his next pamphlet he took a step into the unknown. There was a possibility of a war with Spain. Tone took up the question which had arisen as a matter of form on the regency question. But with the merciless logic which was becoming the habit of his mind as the world around him began to fit into an intelligible pattern, he discerned an issue of real substance. He enquired "Whether Ireland be of right bound to support a war declared by the King of Great Britain on motives and interests purely British?" The legal connection with Britain was in theory confined to the person of the King, though as has been explained the economic and political ties were based on the colonial system which had not been destroyed by the "patriot party". Tone noted that if the King could declare war the British Parliament could decline to vote supplies. Why should the Irish Parliament not do the same? This was the first plea for neutrality in a British war. Tone examined the question not only from its legal aspects but from the standpoint of Irish interest. He wrote:-

> *"It will not be pretended that WE have immediately, from our own concerns, any ground for interfering in the approaching war; on the contrary, peace with all the world, but peace with Spain*

particularly, is OUR object and interest. The quarrel is merely and purely English. A few individuals in China, members of a company which is possessed of the monopoly of the commerce of the East, TO THE UTTER EXCLUSION OF THIS COUNTRY, fitted out certain ships to trade to the North Western coast of America for furs . . . The Spaniards, actuated by pride or jealousy, or both, have, it seems seized these vessels to the disgrace of (not the Irish but) the British flag . . . but . . . unconnected with the interest in question, debarred of the gains of the commerce, what has Ireland to demand her interference more than if the debate arose between the Emperor of Japan and the king of Korea?"

And later he went on:-

We have no quarrel with Spain, no infraction of good faith, no national insult to complain of. No, but we have the resentments of a rapacious English East Indian monopolist to gratify, who at the distance of half the globe, kindles the torch of war amidst the eternal snows of Nootka sound, and hurls it into the bosom of our commerce.'[34]

After listing the quantities of trade with Spain likely to be lost, and puncturing the popular phrase the "good of the Empire" as meaning the good of England, Tone then demanded the establishment of a national flag, and the beginnings of military equality with England. If Ireland required England's "protection," this was because England kept her unarmed. If she threatened to withdraw that protection then, he replied, "let her do so; everything is beneficial to Ireland that throws us on our own strength." It was significant that this pamphlet which urged pushing to its utmost legal limit the constitution of 1782 was signed "Hibernicus."

Tone quickly learned that he had gone in advance of his Dublin contemporaries. The "patriots" paid little heed. "Sir," said an English bishop to his bookseller, "if the principles contained in that abominable work were to spread, do you know that you would have to pay for your coals at the rate of five pounds a ton?" In short, the logic of freedom of trade was separation; but the bourgeoisie were not in a position to apply that logic. Tone credited Swift and Molyneux with converting him to nationalism; but he had in fact passed a century beyond them.

POLITICAL CLUB

About this time Tone became acquainted with Thomas Russell, afterwards his most intimate friend, and tried with his assistance to form a political club to propagate the Radical Whig opinions he had now arrived at. He took a small house in Irishtown which Russell visited together with Tone's father and younger brother who was busy at Brooke's cotton mills at Prosperous, Co. Kildare. Many were the discussions. The club included men who subsequently became famous, notably Thomas Addis Emmet, William Drennan, Burrows and Whitley Stokes. Tone's four essays written for the society show a sharpening intentness on the separate identity of the Irish nation, and the last raised the question of the unity of Protestants, Catholics and Dissenters.

Yet that he had not yet rejected the personal Union of Britain and Ireland seems implicit in his correspondence on the subject of the plan to colonise the Sandwich Islands which he resumed on September 30th. He was opposed to Ireland's making war on Spain but urged that it might be in England's interest to do so.

At this time his opinions seem to have been making their most rapid evolution. For whereas the letter of 30th September concentrates on the commercial advantages which would accrue to England, that of 12th November stresses the "Liberation of South America" whose inhabitants long for their independence since they are "loaded with an unmerciful tax, the King's quinta, devouring one-fifth of their property at every transfer." His final memorial composed in December proposes as the object of the enterprise, "A free Republic in South America, with her liberty guaranteed by England and North America, and a fair and equitable treaty of commerce between the three nations, which would in effect, though not in form exclude the rest of the world."[34]

This proposal draws from Mr MacDermot the comment that "In face of this correspondence, which took place when Tone was in his twenty-eighth year, it is impossible to accept the legend that he had either an instinctive hatred of England or a natural passion for human liberty. The right of the Sandwich Islanders to peace and independence does not seem to have entered his mind. . ." But what the correspondence really shows is, of course, the confused groping after universal liberty of a mind which had not yet freed itself from mercantilism.

At this time the French revolution was in progress but not yet properly understood. It was widely held, in France as elsewhere, that Great Britain might ally itself with the revolution and topple feudal

54

restrictions everywhere. The true content of the French revolution cannot, of course, be found in contemporary consciousness of it. It represented the fall of French feudalism; the upsurge of French capitalism; it was England's Cromwellian revolution expanded in a more advanced age. It became an issue in the internal politics of Britain and Ireland when in October 1790 Burke published his denunciatory *Reflections on the French Revolution* and Thomas Paine (whose pamphlet *Commonsense* had helped to inspire the American revolt) sent out his reply in February 1791. This was the celebrated *Rights of Man*. In the controversy which ensued, abstract as much of it was, the issues of the French Revolution became public property. It was only as a result of this controversy that Tone began to grasp the necessity for a similar revolution in Ireland, and advanced by degrees to the position of Republicanism. So if Tone could not possibly from his class origins have an ''instinctive'' hatred of England, yet through experience he acquired a hatred of the British ruling class. As is usually the case with political sentiments, his passion for human liberty matured as he saw more deeply what it was needed for.

FRENCH REVOLUTION

The French revolution began on 17th June 1789 when the third (bourgeois) estate of the Estates-general, reluctantly called by the king to discuss grievances as the price of securing subsidies, abolished the division of its separate orders and constituted the National Assembly. As in England in 1641, America in 1776, and indeed in Ireland in 1919, a legally constituted assembly appropriated unaccustomed powers.

There is a widespread belief that great revolutions necessarily begin with their loudest bang. History shows that this is not so. The most important precondition for a revolution is not heroism or even good preparations by the revolutionaries, but the inability of the old ruling class to rule longer in the old way.[42]

The change that took place in France seemed first to betoken no more that replacing an absolute monarchy by a constitutional one. That court circles brought in troops and that the people of Paris resisted, attacking the Tuileries and razing the Bastille, was taken as a natural concomitant of the change. But the enormous impetus with which the revolution communicated itself to the country and the energy with which the feudal barriers were cast down by the peasantry, soon made it clear that the French were not going to be contented with the half-measures of seventeenth-century England.

55

Within a year the National Assembly had abolished the privileges of the provincial parliaments, the nobles and the church whose property was nominally transferred to the municipalities but more often finished in the hands of speculators. The civil and judicial code was rewritten on the principle of the "sovereignty of the nation" whose working class none the less suffered restricted rights as (of all things) "passive citizens," but the royal prerogative was swept away in field after field. A stream of refugees left the country.

On 20th June 1791 Louis XIV, emulating James II, fled secretly from the capital. It was widely believed that his purpose was to undertake the leadership of a civil war against the revolution. He was stopped at Varennes and immediately brought back to Paris under arrest. Thereupon there were two trends of opinion, those who advocated the immediate establishment of a Republic and those who thought the time had come to strike a balance. They corresponded roughly to large and small property interests, with the "passive citizens" following the latter.

Edmund Burke, a former Whig with liberal views on Catholic emancipation provided it was confined to the gentry, immediately grasped the danger of French conceptions of popular sovereignty spreading on the less stable soil of England. Still more he dreaded their effect on landlordism in Ireland. He therefore set out to frighten the British property-owning classes, and preached what amounted to a crusade of intervention against revolutionary France. In doing so he stirred up a radical opposition which found a literary champion in Thomas Paine, and organisational form in the London Corresponding Society.[43]

Tone described the impact of the French revolution on Ireland in his memoirs:

> *"The French Revolution had now been above a twelve-month in its progress; at its commencement, as the first emotions are generally honest, everyone was in its favour; but after some time the probable consequences to monarachy and aristocracy began to he foreseen, and the partisans of both to retrench considerably in their admiration: at length Mr Burke's famous invective appeared, and this in due season produced Paine's reply which he called the* Rights of Man.
>
> *"This controversy and the gigantic event which gave rise to it changed in an instant the politics of Ireland. Two years before the nation was in a lethargy . . . But the rapid succession of events,*

56

and above all the explosion which had taken place in France, and blown into the elements a despotism rooted in fourteen centuries, had thoroughly aroused all Europe, and the eyes of every man in every quarter, were turned anxiously on the French National Assembly.

"In England, Burke had the triumph completely to decide the public . . . But matters were very different in Ireland, an oppressed, insulted and plundered nation . . . In a little time the French Revolution became the test of every man's political creed, and the nation was fairly divided into two great parties, the Aristocrats and the Democrats (epithets borrowed from France) who have ever since been measuring each other's strength, and carrying on a kind of smothered war, which the course of events, it is highly probable, may soon call into energy and action . . . It is needless, I believe, to say that I was a Democrat from the very commencement* and as all the retainers of Government, including the sages and judges of the law, were of course on the other side, this gave the coup de grace to any expectations, if any such I had, of my succeeding at the bar."[35]

BELFAST

In the winter of 1790-91, Russell left Dublin for Belfast, and there fell in with the leaders of the Volunteers, who decided to commemorate the fall of the Bastille on July 14th. Thomas Russell invited Tone to draft some resolutions which were presented for approval. They called for a reform of parliament, a reduction of the weight of English influence in the Government, and a "complete internal union of all the people" of Ireland, with measures "tending to the abolition of distinctions between Irishmen." The last provision, a careful and guarded enough advocacy of Catholic emancipation, was subjected to some opposition and its passage was deferred.

Tone wrote in his memoirs that on learning of such hesitation in the centre of Irish radicalism he was "set on thinking more seriously than I had yet done upon the state of Ireland." He went on, "I soon formed my theory and on that theory I have unvaryingly acted ever since."

He was now twenty-eight years old. He had before him a problem which appeared no simpler at that time than does that of Northern

---

*i.e. from the very commencement of the controversy.

Ireland to this generation. He showed the quality of his mind by posing and answering the crucial questions. What was the obstacle to the rebuilding of Ireland which had been destroyed by the invasions? English influence. What kept it there? The disunity of the Irish people. What was the cause of that disunity? The enslavement of the Catholic three-quarters of the population. "My present impression," he wrote on July 17th, "is to become a red hot Catholic, seeing that in the party, apparently, and perhaps really, it is rather a monopoly than an extension of liberty which is their object." By August 1st he had completed a pamphlet called *An argument on behalf of the Catholics of Ireland*, which was published within a month and caused a great sensation. At that time, he records, he was not personally acquainted with a single Catholic.*

He explained his purpose in his memoirs: "To subvert the tyranny of our execrable Government, to break the connection with England, the never failing source of all our political evils, and to assert the independence of my country — these were my objects. To unite the whole people of Ireland, to abolish the memory of all past dissensions, and to substitute the common name of Irishman in place of the denominations of Protestant, Catholic and Dissenter, these were my means."[35] Tone had enunciated clearly the doctrine of Irish nationality. He had given a political solution (not a doctrinaire phrase) to the fundamental political question confronting the Irish people.

POLITICAL SOLUTION

His pamphlet is a model of sober political judgement. He first discredits the revolution of 1782 which has not yielded the fruits desired. He asserts, "We have no national Government," because the principal ministers of state were appointed by the British Prime Minister and were responsible to him alone. He carefully avoids a frontal attack on the crown, professing loyalty to the king while proposing to deprive him of his last vestiges of power. An Irishman should, he says, owe "his first duty to his country, his second to his king." In this way he manoeuvres within existing constitutional forms and only purists will disapprove. He then proposes a reform of Parliament which will place

---

*It might be argued that Northern Ireland today awaits the pen of some Protestant who can grasp that the secret of the power of Unionism in the six counties, with all it entails, lies in the system by which Catholics are in one way or another made second class citizens.

political power in the hands of the people, and asserts that "no reform is honourable, practicable or just, which does not include as a fundamental principle the extension of elective franchise to the Roman Catholics. . . ."[33]

He replies to the current objections, most of which follow lines familiar in our day when applied to the independence of African colonies or the reunification of Ireland — Catholics are not to be trusted, they are ignorant, they are not prepared for liberty, they follow the temporal power of the Pope, they are Jacobites, they will get a majority and attach the country to France. Each argument is neatly answered, and always he comes back to the main question, that only by freeing the Catholic can the Irish Protestant be free himself, free from the necessity of playing second fiddle to the "Honourable United Company of Merchants trading, where he must never trade, to the East Indies;" the clothiers of Yorkshire, the weavers of Manchester, nor yet to the constitution-reforming blacksmiths of Birmingham."*

The first consequences of Tone's pamphlet was his becoming acquainted with the leaders of the Catholics in Dublin, first John Keogh, then Richard McCormick and others. It was well received in Belfast and he was induced to visit the city and meet the members of a "secret committee" whose purpose was to establish an organisation to propagate the views it expressed. Arriving there on 11th October 1791, he was elected a member of the Belfast Volunteers and met the principal men of the city, notably Henry Joy, the Whig leader, Samuel Neilson and the able and enterprising businessman William Sinclair who showed him the most recent industrial developments about the town. He attended the inaugural meeting of the United Irishmen on October 18th, where it was decided to communicate with Napper Tandy and Richard McCormick with the suggestion of a similar society in Dublin.

UNITED IRISHMEN
The first Society of United Irishmen was founded on the three resolutions:

(1) That the weight of English influence in the government of this country is so great as to require a cordial union among all the people

---

*For the honour of Birmingham let it be said that Joseph Priestley ordered several copies of Tone's pamphlet.

of Ireland, to maintain that balance which is essential to the preservation of our liberties and the extension of our commerce.

(2) That the sole constitutional mode by which this influence can be opposed is by a complete and radical reform of the representation of the people in Parliament.

(3) That no reform is practicable, efficacious, or just, which shall not include Irishmen of every religious persuasion.

Back in Dublin Tone participated in the foundation of the Dublin Society on 9th November, with Napper Tandy as secretary and the Hon. Simon Butler as its first chairman. The importance of the establishment of these societies was that thanks to Tone's genius, the mistake of 1783 had now been discovered. Parliamentary reform was essential to parliamentary independence. A revolutionary government spares at its peril the system by which its predecessors held power. Now the weapon had been discovered by which the revolution could be taken to its proper conclusion. The purpose was to make the constitution in actuality what it purported to be in theory, and nobody who reads through the files of the *Northern Star* can mistake this meaning: the constitution was to be defended against those who had perverted it. The means was parliamentary reform. If force were to be used the onus was on the Government in office. In the event the Government proved quite willing to accept the onus.

Tone did not long busy himself with the affairs of the Dublin Society for which others were available who enjoyed the responsibility. Emboldened by the support of the northern Dissenters and the establisment of the United Irishmen in Dublin, the Catholic Committee discussed the possibility of petitioning at once for the repeal of the penal code. Tone had no sooner won over the Dissenters when the Catholics responded. The landed interest in the committee threw every obstacle in the way of the new proposal, but the debate ended in the secession of Lord Kenmare and sixty-eight of the ''leading and respectable'' members, who covered themselves with ridicule by offering the Government their cringing ''eleemosynary address.''

When the petition was presented to Parliament in February 1792 the sixty-eight seceders came forward to deny that the Committee any longer represented the Catholics of Ireland. The committee took a bold and logical step which would have been impossible but for the support they now had in Belfast. They appealed to the Catholic people, and resolved to organise the Catholics of Ireland through primary and secondary assemblies who would thus elect their committee to treat with the Government. Their plan of campaign was published in March 1792 and shortly afterwards Wolfe Tone was engaged as their permanent secretary whose duty was to put the scheme into effect.

CATHOLIC RELIEF

Here was a challenge no government ln Ireland faced before. A stream of resolutions and warnings came from all the organs of the Ascendancy, but the organisation proceeded rapidly. In July Tone was in Belfast once more and suggested that the Dissenters should organise in the same way as the Catholics. The effort was carried into the countryside. For long past agrarian feuds between Catholics and Protestants had been encouraged by the authorities in the mixed counties of south Ulster, above all in Co. Armagh. Signs appeared that efforts were being made to foment those in the Co. Down. Tone and Neilson visited Rathfriland after some disturbances were reported and secured an agreement between the parties. Generally speaking it was found possible to achieve unity where the dominant local forces were bourgeois, but extremely difficult where the landowners ruled the roost. The failure to separate the Protestant peasantry from the Protestant landowners was a serious setback whose full significance only appeared later.

In October Tone visited Galway for the famous Ballinasloe fair which was attended by all the leading Catholics of Connaught. There he persuaded them to support the new organisation. Returning to Dublin he took the sense of his own profession and found the opinion of the bar "marvellously changed" in favour of the Catholics. The Catholic Convention met in Back Lane, Dublin, on December 2nd at a time when everything was in their favour. The Government was taken by surprise at the rapid growth of Catholic organisation. The invading Prussians were being driven out of France where the king had been deposed. And in anticipation of war Pitt's administration in England was anxious for conciliation. It was decided to take the unprecedented step of by-passing the Dublin administration and taking the petition for emancipation direct to the king.

Owing to unfavourable weather conditions it was necessary to take the short sea route from Larne, which involved passing through Belfast.

61

Here an amazing spectacle was seen. When the Catholic delegates came into the town the leading citizens, all Dissenters, took the horses from between the shafts and drew the carriages through the town with their own hands amid scenes of intense enthusiasm. After some difficulties with the secretary, Dundas, the delegates obtained an audience with the king on January 2nd, were promised that relief would be recommended in the speech from the throne, and assured that England "desired approbation and support from them only in proportion to the measure of relief afforded."

TRAPPED

When the Irish Parliament met on January 10th 1793, the Lord Lieutenant's speech contained recommendations indeed, but couched in somewhat vague terms. Some of Tone's papers published by his son suggest that one of the delegates to London held private conversations with the Home Secretary and was persuaded to consent to a plan for less than complete emancipation.[34] The British had played on the Catholic landlords' fear of their tenants. The Committee, to Tone's intense indignation and disappointment, fell into the trap. Asked what measure of relief was wanted, instead of replying that they desired complete equality with other sects, they agreed to enter into negotiations. The Government was enabled to protract these while sapping the confidence of the Catholics and undermining the unity of the national movement. As Philip Harwood put it:-

> "There was deep and dexterous policy in Mr Pitt's management of this Catholic question in 1793. Enough was given to take off the edge of popular discontent, to thin the ranks of disaffection, and save Ireland to the empire; yet what was given was so given as to damp the people's confidence in themselves and their leaders, depress the tone of popular feeling, and break the strength of any new popular movement."[30]

Nevertheless the Relief Act of 1793 was the most substantial measure of Catholic emancipation ever given. Industry and property were freed from the restraints of the penal code. Catholics were enabled to enter the army, navy and university, serve on juries, to become magistrates and members of corporations. The elective franchise was given them. But they were denied the right to sit in Parliament, and debarred from the shrievalty and the high offices of state.

The Ascendancy had been forced to make a major retreat. They had saved their predominance because the Catholics could still vote only for their enemies. Yet the power to vote at all was a strong one and its ultimate results were unforeseeable. From January 1793 Dublin Castle was imbued with one idea only, counter-revolution, and it is to the eternal infamy of William Pitt that he assisted them to batter Ireland's independent Parliament to death on the faces of the Irish people.

4

War and Reaction

It is doubtful whether the Ascendancy would have achieved its object, or indeed William Pitt his, but for favourable circumstances which arose from extraneous causes. The course of the revolution in France steadily thrust apart the compromising "constitutionalists" from the more democratic parties. The Constitutionalists were ousted in favour of a Girondin ministry in March 1792, and after some exchanges, war was declared on Austria on April 20th. Prussia joined the war in July, the Duke of Brunswick publishing on the 27th[44] a warning that Paris would suffer from his vengeance if it injured the King and Queen, together with other threats which provoked French indignation to fever-heat.

On August 10th vast crowds swarmed round the Tuileries demanding the deposition of the King. The Swiss guards were overborne and the palace was sacked. The Legislative Assembly, now entirely Girondin and Jacobin, suspended the king's functions, placed him and the queen under arrest, and summoned a national convention, elected by universal manhood suffrage.

The conscript army, drawn from the lower orders, was so heartened by the success of the uprising that it won the historic victory of Valmy, on September 2nd. A mass levy was decreed to clear the frontiers of the invaders, and by the end of the year revolutionary France had confounded all her enemies. The discovery of documents which connected Louis XVI with the invasion, led to his trial and subsequent execution on January 21st 1793. It is true of course that there were excesses committed though it is also true that they lost nothing in the telling. But to "respectable" opinion all Burke had said now seemed justified.

This situation seemed to offer Pitt his best opportunity to declare war. Should it seem inconsistent that the English with their rooted habit of chasing kings from their thrones should go to war to restore monarchy

64

in France, reference must be had to the solid economic motives which existed, the keeping of the Continent open to British trade and the smothering of a potential industrial rival.

There were internal motives also. A stronger pro-French party than is usually admitted had established itself in Britain. It included moderate and radical Whigs, but also a considerable body of working class, lower middle class and professional opinion. For some twenty years there had been a strong movement for electoral reform in Britain. Its urgency is shown from the fact that Manchester with a population of 50,000 had no representation in Parliament at all. Neither did Birmingham or Sheffield. But Old Sarum, a grassy mound four miles north of New Sarum or Salisbury, returned two Members. As early as 1780 the "London Society for Constitutional Information" had been set up with the object of changing this state of affairs. Among its members were Horne Tooke, John Wilkes's most able lieutenant, Dr. Jebb and Major Cartwright. Among the "dissenting radicals" was Dr. Joseph Priestly, the discoverer of oxygen. The earlier societies took on a new lease of life after 1789 and the first distinctly plebeian organisation, the London Corresponding Society, was founded on 25th January 1792.

The middle class leaders of the radicals gathered increasing working-class support during the later years of the eighteenth century. The industrial revolution was gathering way in England and to the discontent of ruined handicraft men and evicted peasants was added the more permanent rebellion of factory operatives who sought protection from sweated conditions in strikes, which sometimes led to riots, arson and machine- breaking.[43] The execution of Louis XVI enabled Pitt to drive a wedge into the Whig-radical alliance with its working-class connections, and when this was done he was in a position to wage an internal war against the English common people in the interests of the landlords and employers. He did not scruple to make full use of the spy, the informer and the agent provocateur.[45]

Wolfe Tone fully appreciated the reactionary character of Pitt's war. When the news came of the execution of Louis XVI he commented laconically, "I am sorry it was necessary." When the personal Union was urged to bring Ireland into conflict not with Spain but revolutionary France, he stated clearly that such a war was not in the interests of Ireland:

"We are going to war with France; very well; now the first question I would ask is, what quarrel have we with France? What did she ever do to us or we to her? 'Why, the French cut off the King's head.' That to be sure is very shocking and barbarous, and I for one am heartily sorry for it; but will our going to war put it on again; or what right have we to meddle in their disputes while they let us alone? I remember to have read that the English cut off King Charles's head just as the French did their King's, but I do not find that any nation in Europe was so foolish as to go to war with them on that score. What was Ireland the better of the King of France when he was alive or what is she the worse of him now that he is dead?"

As for the accusation that the French were Republicans and Levellers, Tone proceeds:

"I am sure a great many of us make use of these words that do not know the meaning of them. But suppose they are levellers and republicans and suppose that these words mean everything that is wicked and abominable, still, I say, what is that to us? If a Republic is a bad form of government, in God's name let them have it and punish themselves; if it be a good form, I do not know what right we have to hinder it."

THE NORTHERN STAR

Soon after the establishment of the United Irishmen, Samuel Neilson founded their official organ, the *Northern Star*, whose columns reported not only the deliberations of the French Assembly, in extenso, but the resolutions of the corresponding societies in England and Scotland. Thus it is recorded that the Society of the Friends of the People held their first meeting at the Freemasons' Tavern, London, on April 26th 1792. The proceedings were reported in full. The "Constitutional Society" of Manchester the "Friends of Universal Peace and Harmony" in Stockport, whose resolution condemned the war against France, the "Friends of the People" in Edinburgh, and the "Society for Constitutional Information" which met at the Talbot Inn, Derby, were given prominence. This last resolved not only against the poor representation of the people but against "high taxes and the frequency of wars."[46]

The educational range of the *Northern Star* was extensive. There were extracts from Paine and Godwin and accounts of political conditions in far-away Poland and Lithuania. There were attacks on the slave trade, the game laws and the "barbarous art of boxing." Its reports of meetings must cover only a fraction of those that took place. But they came from such various parts as Belfast, Lisburn, Newry, Newtownards, Saintfield, Ballymena, Ballymoney, Toome, Cookestown, Dungannon, Enniskillen and Coleraine. Meetings in Dublin were reported, and the detail appertaining to Wexford should dispose of the erroneous notion that the United Irishmen had little influence in that county.

The *Northern Star* showed no alarm at the rising of August 10th. The "September massacres" however caused great disquiet, and for one or two issues the sentiment of the paper was almost anti-French. After correspondents had joined in polemics, the Convention replaced the Assembly in the paper, and neither the establishment of the Republic nor the execution of the king seems to have wrung its withers to any serious degree. One or two declarations were preceded by assurances of "abhorrence of republican forms of government in this country," but from references in Tone's diary and other evidence it is plain that when France became a republic many United Irishmen became republicans with it. Belfast sentiment was entirely sound; it baulked at the massacre of people, but accepted the execution of a tyrant after process of law.

Apart from an extremely enthusiastic reception for Napper Tandy in Lurgan, which seems to have encouraged the romantic streak in his nature, no movement is reported in the County Armagh. As has been pointed out, this county was the Achilles heel of Ulster. Here the most deliberate policy had been pursued over years by the landed gentry, of putting up tenancies to auction through middlemen, and in particular setting Catholic and Protestant tenants bidding against each other. There was some cottage industry in the county, and it is stated that Protestants were extremely reluctant to see Catholics in the weaving business.[47] The struggles of Protestant and Catholic tenants against the landlords had been diverted into mutually destructive sectarianism, in which, however it is only right to record that the Protestants were nearly always the aggressors, and their aggression was connived at by the authorities.

Another division in the ranks of the radicals, that between workers and employers, is of general rather than immediate interest. The

Northern Star of June 9th 1792 reported that "a very bold and daring spirit of combination has broken out among the cotton weavers, and has been communicated to the bricklayers. It behoves the master artisans in these branches to take such measures as to bring the question in a proper manner before the public, and not individually yield to demands made in a tumultuous and illegal manner."

The *Northern Star* then called on the Volunteers to "enforce the law" and "preserve order." Strikes (combinations) were of course illegal, and cotton weavers were being paid six shillings a week,[48] linen workers somewhat less. A town's meeting was called, among others by Samuel Neilson and William Sinclair, the subject being "What is to be done about combinations?" At the meeting a proposal was made that a commitee of three journey-men, three masters and three "disinterested inhabitants" should "fix proper standard prices for each trade." It was lost and the Sovereign (mayor) instead read extracts from the Combination Acts and praised the Volunteers. What is interesting is not so much the decision to stand firm against the workers, but the proposal, so out of keeping with the times, to put the matter to arbitration.

A further "assembly of the working people" was reported in the following November. A very rapid rise in prices had taken place which was believed to arise from excessive exports and the operation of "forestallers." Finding no grain on board any of the ships, the workers threatened to enter warehouses and seize supplies. "Friends of Liberty" distributed leaflets that night and the workers went home. *The Star* suggested that the way to end such demonstrations was to "remove the cause" and by prohibiting forestallers and regraters from entering the market to allow farmer and consumer to meet and deal at a fair price.[46]

The proletariat had registered its independent existence. The most far-sighted of the Ascendancy must have glimped in this new class whose interests were everywhere the same the strongest force of all for national unity. Their general reaction was irritation against the growing turbulence of Jacobin Belfast.

THE CATHOLICS TRICKED

The aim of the administration was, while preserving undiminished the power of the landlord class, to divide the opposition by depriving it of every focus of agitation, and under cover of concessions which were inconclusive in themselves, disarm the Volunteers, embody a militia answerable only to the authority of the ruling class, destroy the right of assembly, abolish freedom of the press, and finally by involving the United Irishmen in suspicion of preparations for armed uprising prepare the way for their suppression.

The error of the Catholic committee in accepting less than complete emancipation greatly assisted Lord Fitzgibbon as director of government operations. What the Catholics had given up was the prospect of ruling the country in association with the Dissenters. They had rejected the revolution which alone could safeguard their future position, alarming the ruling oligarchy without destroying its power. Machiavelli counselled "either make a man your friend or put it beyond his power to be your enemy." This maxim the Catholic Committee had sadly neglected.

The Catholic Relief Bill had been imposed on the administration by the wider interests of the Imperial Government. Means were contrived to delay its passage until April 9th, some of the gag acts being taken through their stages pari passu. A most humiliating restriction embodied in it, and there were sixteen in all, was the necessity for a Catholic who wished to avail himself of its concessions to swear an oath in the form:-

> "I, A.B. do hereby declare that I do profess the Roman Catholic religion. I, A.B. do swear that I do abjure, condemn and detest, as unchristian and impious the principle that it is lawful to murder, destroy, or any ways injure any person whatsoever, for, or under the pretence of being a heretic . . . . I also declare that it is not an article of the Catholic faith, neither am I thereby required to believe or profess that the Pope is infallible, or that I am bound to obey an order in its own nature immoral, though the Pope or any ecclesiastical power should issue or direct such order, but on the contrary, I hold that it would be sinful in me to pay any respect or obedience thereto. . ." and so on ad nauseam.[29]

This was a gratuitous insult from an administration fully conscious of its own hypocrisy.

The Catholic Committee could have remained united in support of a whole measure, as Tone untiringly argued, but a compromise gave scope for a whole spectrum of attitudes and reservations. The Ulster convention at Dungannon in February went by with scarce a ripple of interest, and the Dissenters who had borne the heat and burden of the struggle felt betrayed and isolated. Bills which had been rejected when proposed by Grattan were introduced or promised by the administration, as further sweets before the pills that were to come. They included a Responsibility Bill, a Place Bill, and a Pension Bill, but no general reform. There was also provision for opening trade with the East Indies, and concessions for those wishing to improve barren land.

'FRENCH PLOT'

The teeth were in the Bills which passed simultaneously, while the Catholics were held in the bog of indecisive negotiations. Fitzgibbon professed to smell the emanations of a desperate French plot, and instituted a Secret Committee of the Lords to bring its perpetrators into a "Star Chamber." Then came a Gunpowder Act, whose very title would cause alarm. It provided for the licensing of imports of that material (which might of course be used by the desperadoes of the "French plot") and, more to the point, the forbidding of the holding of arms without licence. Some flamboyant demonstrations of the "National Guard", whose founder, Napper Tandy, seemed to imagine himself living in France* despite Tone's warnings, added grist to Fitzgibbon's mill. Drennan's call for a civil and military convention with the words "Citizen soldiers, to arms," added point to the scare, and Hamilton Rowan, who had presided at the meeting where it was approved, was prosecuted for sedition.

The Government seized the artillery of Tandy's "Liberty Corps" and secured by agreement the arms of the merchants and lawyers. Warnings against similar action in Belfast were published in the *Northern Star*. Dragoons were sent into Belfast and the Volunteers of that city were in turn overpowered. Neilson sent full accounts to Dublin, but the Catholic Committee did not respond. They were anxious not to "jeopardise the Bill" by challenging the Government. The mass of the Catholics in the country felt leaderless and "sulked". The mistake of 1783 had been repeated after all. A revolution had been begun but not pursued. And the democrats had not come to grips with the new situation.

---

*Some members of the Society of United Irishmen had taken to calling each other "Citizen." Tone's caustic comment was "Make yourselves free and call yourselves what you please. But you are no more citizens for . . . calling yourselves by that name than you would all be peers and nobles by calling each other 'My Lord'."

In December 1792, before the Catholic delegates had gone to London, Fitzgibbon had decided how to deal with them. He had made proposals for embodying a militia. An Act for this purpose was passed while the Relief Bill was under discussion, and now that the Volunteers were in effect disbanded there ended what had been a species of dual power. John Mitchel wrote:-

"The new Militia law was one of the most efficient of that series of measures now secured by the Government to enable them at any time to crush down any popular movement which was not to their taste."

Finally, delayed till July by Whig opposition, came the Convention Act, also envisaged the previous December. It was said at first to aim at preventing riots arising from "tumultuous conventions." Then riots were forgotten about and the Bill was to prevent the United Irishmen's convention at Athlone, this being part of the "French Plot." On Grattan's pointing out that no such convention was in contemplation its real reason was exposed. It was to prevent freedom of assembly in general, put a stop to Catholic conventions in particular, and above all to prevent the United Irishmen constituting themselves a legal mass opposition party. It was still being used to restrict public assembly half a century later.[29]

The administration took advantage of the difficulties of the popular movement to hound and harass individual members of the Society of United Irishmen, to occupy the attention of the movement while they embodied the militia which was to be their salvation. Agrarian disturbances obligingly occurred early in the year, and the threat of associating them with the Catholic Committee was held over the head of that body. Napper Tandy was accused of illegal oath-taking and fled the country in May. Simon Butler and Oliver Bond were sentenced to a large fine and six months' imprisonment for daring to suggest that Fitzgibbon's measures were unconstitutional.

RESISTANCE

Despite their successes the administration did not have it all their own way. In April 1793 the preparations for the militia had been made. But it required all the resources of Government to carry its decision into effect. The opposition of the peasantry was so intense that in many counties resistance bordered on civil war.[49] The north was comparatively quiet, except for the Co. Down. Resistance was strongest in Leitrim, Sligo and Roscommon, but by no means confined to these counties. It was substantial in Mayo, Clare, Kerry, Meath and Fermanagh. Pitched battles were fought at Ballinafad, Athboy and Enniskillen. At Wexford conscripts were rescued by force, and there were successful refusals to perform service in Co. Wicklow. The resistance was partly economic, partly instinctive opposition to serving under the officership of the landlords, and squireens, and partly also a fear of being sent to fight abroad.

In Connaught the notorious Lord Carhampton instituted his own courts-martial and in defiance of all law carted off those who protested and had them impressed into the British Navy. Parliament later passed a Bill of Indemnity for his protection. In the end the militia was embodied, but its rank and file were unwilling soldiers and for long their loyalty was doubtful. The administration had unintentionally achieved another dangerous thing for which they were to pay. They had drawn the mass of the peasantry together not merely for local agrarian defence, but in favour of a national principle. After a hundred years, and under new and advanced conditions, the spirit of the septs became alive again.

The Catholic Committee decided to suspend agitation following the passage of the Relief Act, thus offering the completion of its work to such of the Whigs as cared to pursue it. They kept in being an organisation which was mainly concerned with settling the accounts of the late agitation. Tone was publicly thanked and voted £1,500 for his services. In deference to the wishes of the Dissenters the Committee voted a resolution on Parliamentary reform, but failed to express thanks to the Dissenters for their help. As in 1783 agitation, blocked in its main line of advance, turned down side channels. This has happened repeatedly in Irish history.

In August 1793, Samuel Neilson wrote to Richard McCormick bitterly complaining that the contribution of the Northerners had been forgotten at a celebration dinner to honour Lord Moira:-

> *"Will you excuse an unfortunate persecuted northern incendiary the liberty of asking once more his reputed countryman and friend one simple question? Is Ireland abandoned? I mean by those who have the necessary abilities and confidence to lead the great majority of the Catholics; if so let us all join in the act. We once united, or appeared to unite, in an effort to resue our common country.*

She has not been rescued.
Where lies the Cause? Who are in fault?"

After sarcastically placing the responsibility at the door of the Dissenters he went on:-

"I will repeat it, the meeting at Daly's insulted the Province of Ulster; because, when ransacking the very dregs of royalty, aristocracy and pseudo-patriotism for toasts, they tacitly condemned one-fourth of their countrymen, the body who saved them, when deserted or opposed by all those whom they toasted on the 20th instant. Your prudence in overlooking Mr Tandy, who has been destroyed in your cause; your wisdom in disregarding the sufferings of Mr. Butler, Bond and Reynolds, who were imprisoned for you; and your temperance in neglecting this town which has been abandoned this four months past to martial law on your account, cannot but be highly gratifying to every true Irishman. But your omitting to mention the Dungannon Convention, which represented one million and a quarter of your countrymen, and which demanded the restoration of your rights in particular . . I confess I can never forget."

These strong words had an effect on McCormick who sent the letter on to Tone saying that Neilson's "complaints and heavy charges" were "some exaggerated, but in general too well founded." He was going to Newry and would push on to Belfast in hopes of meeting him and satisfying him.³⁴ The leaders of the Catholic Committee now realised they had been tricked. The manacle had been loosened on one wrist only to be more attached to the other. The discontent among the peasantry and the representations of the Dissenters brought them to a realisation of the mistake that had been made. The fault was reparable, if tackled quickly.

By the end of the year discussions were once more afoot. Tone and Russell approached Keogh with proposals for recovering the position. They were not sanguine at the start, for though Keogh had now realised his mistake and was anxious to resume action, McCormick blamed Keogh for being taken in by the British and at first declined to co-operate. Impatient alike with north and south, Tone told his friend that the only hope was from the "sans-culottes" — having in mind no doubt the peasants who had so courageously resisted the militia. There were moves to introduce a further relief Bill and more talk of reform.

Now the United Irishmen published their own programme which included manhood suffrage, annual elections, equal electoral districts, the removal of the property qualification, and payment of members. The mind of Irish democracy became increasingly turned towards France, where Robespierre had established himself and the army was winning fresh victories everyday. "The French, establishing their victory, will free us in spite of ourselves," wrote Russell.[40]

PITT AGAINST THE PEOPLE

In Britain the ruling classes had been thrown into panic. Riots were instigated against prominent reformers. Thomas Paine was threatened with proceedings for the mysterious offence of "seditious libel" and, escaping to France, was tried in his absence in December 1792. About the same time the Scottish Jacobins held a conference in Edinburgh attended by Hamilton Rowan. Its leading spirit, Thomas Muir, was then charged with recommending the works of Thomas Paine and reading a "treasonable address" from the United Irishmen. A further convention was held in November 1793, Gerrald, the delegate from the London Corresponding Society, being arrested and brought to trial. In his defence he offered the argument that Jesus Christ was a reformer. "Muckle he made of that," said the judge, "he was hangit." Spies and agent provocateurs multiplied, together with Acts to suppress sedition, "protect property", and put down treasonable assemblies. The trials of Hamilton Rowan and Dr Drennan in January 1794 fitted into the pattern.[42]

It was in pursuit of this crusade against the common people that Pitt, learning that efforts were being made by the French to make contact in Ireland, attached the spy Cockayne to the entourage of Rev. William Jackson, who visited Dublin on their behalf. The result was what was called "a voyage of discovery in search of treason, under the superintendence of Mr. Pitt, who allowed his emissary to proceed to Ireland, not to detect a conspiracy but to form one, and thus increase the dupes of one party and the victims of another — a singular instance of perfidy and cruelty."[30] The visitors arrived on 1st April 1794. Their first contact was the barrister Leonard McNally, who figured so discreditably in the ruin of Robert Emmet, but who was then believed to be an enthusiastic United Irishman. Jackson and Cockayne won the confidence of Rowan, then a prisoner in Newgate, and at his request

Tone met them and gave Jackson a statement which expressed the incautious opinion that a French invasion in sufficient force would receive the support of the Irish people. To Tone's indignation he learned that copies of the statement had been made. Worse was to follow when one of the copies was intercepted on its way to the Continent and on April 28th Jackson was arrested. Tone was heavily compromised, but despite Whig attempts to persuade the Catholic Committee to disown him, they refused to do so. It was agreed that in return for a statement of what had transpired, in which the names of none of his associates were to be mentioned, he was to be left unmolested. But he must give an undertaking to leave Ireland.

He would probably have left very shortly, but for the British Government running into fresh difficulties. The expected attack on the United Irishmen came on May 4th. Police seized the Taylors' Hall in Back Lane, dispersed the members present there, seized their papers and pronounced the society dissolved. Exactly a week later, the London Corresponding Society and the Constitutional Society were similarly treated. Horne Tooke and five other leaders were arrested and brought to trial. But London was not Edinburgh. Juries refused to convict and by early autumn it was clear that the Government could only pursue its course at the expense of inviting a reaction.

Its policy therefore changed. An alliance with the moderate, or "Old Whigs," was struck, part of the bargain being that wealthier Catholics in Ireland should be conciliated, with a view to creating a front of property-owners throughout the two kingdoms, and isolating the United Irishmen as a preparation for effecting the Union. Under these circumstances the very worst policy would have been to begin by arresting the honoured and successful agent of the Catholic Committee. It was thus to the Catholics that Tone owed his safety and he expressed his gratitude on several occasions.

The new coalition in Britain despatched an "Old Whig" viceroy, Earl Fitzwilliam, who arrived in Dublin on January 4th 1795. Defying Fitzgibbon, he won great popularity by announcing an extensive programme of reform including the completion of Catholic emancipation. Tone was busily engaged drafting petitions and memoranda and accompanied a further deputation to London.

But Fitzgibbon secured a recall of Fitzwilliam through a personal visit to King George III, whose religious mania opened him to the suggestion that agreeing to the complete emancipation of the Catholics would be a breach of his coronation oath. The result was a further Cabinet crisis. Fitzwilliam left Ireland on March 25th. A large concourse of leading citizens dressed in black saw him on board. Ireland was left to the mercy of Beresford, Toler and Fitzgibbon, who were preparing their regime of martial law and military executions. Fitzgibbon became Lord Clare as a reward for this tergiversation. As soon as Fitzwilliam was decently out of the way, Jackson, who had spent a year in jail, was brought up for trial. The Act relating to treason in England prescribed that two witnesses were required for a conviction. But the English Act did not apply in Ireland. Legal precedent was unhesitatingly established that in Ireland only one was required. That one was Pitt's creature Cockayne.

Jackson was convicted on the word of the agent provocateur and brought up for judgement on April 30th. Sentence was about to be pronounced when he collapsed from arsenic poisoning. As he lay in his death agonies Judge and Attorney-General exchanged high legal argument over whether he was in a sufficient state of sensibility to understand the sentence about to be pronounced upon him. It was his corpse that was ordered to be "remanded until further orders".

After this gruesome interlude it was clear to Tone that he must be gone quickly. Fitzgibbon's power was becoming absolute and Tone proposed to offer him no invitation to use it. McCormick and Keogh, now reconciled, secured him the sum of £300 as well as the arrears due to him from the Catholic Committee, and on May 20th 1795 he set off for Belfast. Tone spoke gratefully of the backing given him in Dublin, where he discussed his future action with Russell and Thomas Addis Emmet in Emmet's "triangular field." Of Belfast he wrote: "Even those who scarcely knew me were eager to entertain us; parties and excursions were every day engaged by one or another. On the first Russell, Neilson, Simms, McCracken and one or two more of us, on the summit of McArt's fort, took a solemn obligation — which I think I may say I have on my part endeavoured to fulfil — never to desist in our efforts until we have subverted the authority of England over our country and asserted her independence". The farewell party was entertained by the brilliant songwriter Bunting, whose memory is so unjustly neglected.

Just before Tone left Dublin, that is on May 10th 1795 , the Society of United Irishmen or the "Union" as it came to be called, was reorganised "on a rebellious basis", with the purpose of establishing

"Republican Government and a separation from England." Keogh and the leaders of the Catholic Committee were aware of, and gave their approval to, the great project now in hand.

5

Race Against Time

The reorganisation of the United Irishmen was a turning-point in Irish history. For the first time the Irish nation was exclusively identified with the Irish democracy. The leaders set to work establishing their groups throughout the country. Some of the new members were former Volunteers; it is on record that very few Volunteers were embodied into the militia. Certainly the society from now on possessed a more distinctively plebeian character. An illustrative example is that of James Hope, who was approached by his neighbours in Hightown and invited to join the Society on 26th June 1795. A journeyman weaver, he was warned by no less a person than Henry Joy McCracken against the merchant magnates of Belfast who would see Ireland sunk in the sea rather than have the trade of the western ports expand at the expense of the north-east. For James Hope's part he held the opinion that "so long as men of rank and fortune lead a people, they will modify abuses, reform to a certain extent, but they will never remove any real grievances that press down on the people." Rising high in the councils of the Ulstermen he was later sent to Dublin with the express mission of organising the weavers into the Society.[41] The United Irishmen had not yet reached the point where they defined the anti-national forces precisely in terms of a class, though that was to come from the most advanced of them. The link between Ireland and Britain was the big landed interest, and until the landlord class of Ireland was utterly smashed economically as well as politically, England would always have a garrison. The landlords were rich and powerful and knit together by the guilt of crimes committed in consort. They were in possession of a powerful state apparatus with soldiers of the line and militia on one side and on the other a system of bribery, subornation, intimidation and press-control that would do credit to many a despot of our own day. Standing in reserve was the British Government which decided overall policy, supplied troops and even appointed at pleasure the main executive officers. Outside Belfast (and even there, stratification existed) the desire of the bourgeoisie for future capitalist expansion was balanced to some degree by present links of dependence on the landlords, who having the greatest wealth were naturally the greatest spenders. It was clear to Tone who later impressed it on the French, that a successful rising was impossible without French aid. This was necessary not only because of the forces at the disposal of the administration, but to bring over the waverers, and give the people the confidence to unite. The United Irishmen repeatedly warned against any kind of premature or partial insurrection, and it is difficult to agree with those who sought to blame them because they "waited too long."

DISUNITING THE PEOPLE

The interest of the Government was of course precisely the opposite, namely to disarm, disunite and confuse the people, and insofar as they were able to resist, to waste their energies in indecisive struggles which would afford the excuse for repression. John Mitchel said plainly that from Pitt's point of view it was "no rebellion, no union." But the one type of rebellion which neither Britain nor the Dublin administration dare contemplate was that in which the people rose as one man at the signal of the French landing. This conflict of interest gives the key to the complex development of 1795-97, and the tragic heroic year of 1798. Sectarian strife in the Co. Armagh had been muted during the latter part of 1793 and 1794. It flared up again conveniently when Fitzwilliam arrived. Fitzgibbon and Beresford had circulated the rumour that the new Viceroy was charged with the duty of replacing Protestant ascendancy with Catholic ascendancy. The attacks on the United Irishmen in Dublin were followed up by searches of Catholic homes in Armagh for "seditious literature." The "Peep o' day boys" improved on this by searching Catholic houses for arms (which they were legally entitled to possess), and perpetrating outrages on the families whether they possessed them or not. The Catholic "Defenders" organisation was called into action and very soon the Co. Armagh was showing the signs of civil war. The authorities threw all their weight against the Defenders and the Peep o' day Boys went all but scot free.

"The object of the Armagh disturbances," said Grattan, "was the extermination of all the Catholics of that county. It was a persecution conceived in the bitterness of bigotry, carried out with the most ferocious barbarity, by a banditti who, being of the religion of the state, had committed with the greater audacity and confidence the most horrid murders, and had proceeded from robbery and massacre to extermination; they had repealed by their own authority all the laws lately passed in favour of the Catholics, had established instead of those laws, the inquisition of a mob, resembling Lord George Gordon's fanatics, equalling them in outrage, and surpassing them far in perseverance and success."

THE ORANGE ORDER

It was at this time that, in order to counter the United Irishmen's policy of "Union", the Orange Order was founded on the principle of disunion. The official history of the Order denies that it took its origin from the "Peep o'day boys." Whatever about that, it replaced them and did their work better than they had ever done it themselves. The first Orange lodge was established at Loughgall immediately after an event known as the "Battle of the Diamond." According to Orange mythology[50] "Protestants" were attacked by a force of "defenders" and after performing almost inconceivable acts of heroism repulsed the invaders and drove them back. But one suspicious circumstance admitted in the official account is that "How many were wounded in the rebel host no-one, except themselves, could tell; but they were roughly estimated at fifty. But one Protestant was injured." The facts are that a meeting of Catholics in the hills was sniped at by Protestant sharp-shooters. There was some desultory fighting which was ended by the joint intervention of a Protestant magistrate and a Catholic priest. A further skirmish followed a misunderstanding but peace was restored once more. The Catholics were practically unarmed. The disparity in casualties was thus no miracle, and resolutions of protest at the provocation were passed by the Dissenters of Co. Down.

That night the Orange Order was started. But far from being a "Protestant" organisation in the proper sense of the word, its purpose from the start was to split the Protestants. This purpose was maintained after the rising of 1798 when every Orange candidate took an oath that "I, A.B., solemnly and sincerely swear that I was not, am not, nor will ever be, an United Irishman and that I never took the oath of secrecy to that Society."

"In evaluating the Orange Society,"wrote T. A. Jackson," it must not be forgotten that the bodies it was founded to disrupt and

80

destroy — the United Irishmen and the Defenders — functioned the one as a great liberating force, and the other as a tenants' protection league and an agrarian trade union. The Orange lodges functioned as a 'union-smashing' force, operating in the interest of an oligarchical clique threatened with overthrow by a revolutionary-democratic advance."

This opinion is confirmed by one of their own rules, namely:-

"That we will aid and assist all magistrates and all High and Petty constables in the lawful execution of their office when called on."

What did such office consist of? In Co. Armagh Catholic tenants with good farms found notices posted to their doors saying "To hell or Connaught." If they failed to get out they were burnt out. Within the year commencing with the Battle of the Diamond, no less than seven thousand persons were killed or driven from their homes in the one county. The Orange historians do not produce a single instance of one of their own men being prosecuted. There were one or two cases including one where an Orangeman guilty of murder was released. But on the other hand, the Catholics who were sent wandering the hills without means of support were mercilessly rounded up and imprisoned and their young men sent without ceremony into the British Navy. The fortunate ones were those who escaped to Belfast where they were given work by the Dissenters. The system of outrage against the law was euphemistically described as "vigour beyond the law." Once more Lord Carhampton had a hand in it.

GOVERNMENT TERROR

As the new year opened it became clear that it was Government policy to extend the repression throughout the whole country. In order to facilitate this, two Acts were passed in the winter of 1796 which amounted in sum to the declaration of martial law. The excesses of the Orangemen and the partiality of the Government had led to a swing of public opinion in favour of the United Irishmen. Lord Camden, who succeeded Fitzwilliam as Viceroy, announced that additional powers were required to defeat "dangerous secret societies."

The Attorney-General then introduced an "Indemnity Bill" the purpose of which was "for indemnifying such magistrates and others who might have, since lst January 1795, exceeeded the ordinary forms and rules of law for the preservation of the public peace and suppression of insurrection prevailing in some parts of this kingdom.'' The other bill, the Insurrection Bill, was for the ''more effectual prevention of insurrections, tumults, and riots by persons styling themselves Defenders, and other disorderly persons.'' The new laws' real purpose was shown in supplementary resolutions giving magistrates enlarged powers of arrest and search for arms. ''Defenders'' was merely a scare word to keep the smaller landlords and bigger bourgeois in line. The purpose was to break up the growing strength of the United Irishmen.

Once the Insurrection Act was in operation there would be no need for indemnities. It would legitimate every illegality beforehand. It ''struck the poor out of the protection of the law, the rich out of its penalties.'' The administration of illegal oaths became a ''felony of death'' — not ''treason'' because in a treason trial the defendant's counsel was entitled to address the jury. A majority of seven magistrates were entitled to declare any county in a ''state of insurrection.'' Any two magistrates might authorise the breaking open of any house at any hour of the day or night in search of arms, likewise to imprison any man whom they might find absent from his house between sunset and sunrise, to arrest all vagrants having no visible means of livelihood or othwerwise suspected and send them on board the King's fleet.''

It is evidence of the sharpening class character of the conflict now being joined that on the night the Indemnity and Insurrection Bills were introduced, a motion by John Philpot Curran for appointing a committee to enquire into ''the state of the poor and the wages of labour'' was rejected by a majority of ten to one. Nothing was said about the events in Armagh. This county was not even enumerated among the disturbed districts. The houghing of Protestant bullocks in the south was made more of than the murder of Catholic men and women in the North.

It was as a consequence of the mounting reign of terror that some of the more far-sighted members of the ruling class began not only to detach themselves from the policy of the administration, but even in certain cases to join the United Irishmen. Two notable instances were those of Lord Edward Fitzgerald, and Arthur O'Connor, uncle of the chartist leader. In the same period came Dr. MacNeven of the Catholic Committee and Thomas Addis Emmet; even the shrewd John Keogh cautiously connected himself with the Society.

But when Parliament re-assembled on October 13th 1796, the administration was fully aware that far from weakening the United

Irishmen their repression had driven people to join them out of sheer desperation. A Bill to suspend Habeas Corpus was introduced at 2 a.m. on the 14th, read a first time at five past the hour, read a second time at ten past and was in committee at 2.15. At this rate of despatch it was law next day.

Three days later Grattan's last effort for Catholic emancipation failed, and the unreality of the whole proceeding seems to have begun to dawn on him. Every relief the Catholics had ever won in the legislature was negatived by the practice of the executive. "We shall trouble you no more," he told the House. With Curran and his fellow Whigs he seceded from Parliament and declined to be nominated at the next General Election. Keogh had long urged this course upon him, saying that he should quit the house and come among the people. He was independent enough to do the first, but too much of a gentleman for the second. There now remained no moderating influence, no intercessor or go-between bridging the separation of rulers and people. But in the background was the British Government, making no effort to discourage the Irish Government from incurring odium, but ready to come forward against it once it had crushed the people.

TONE IN FRANCE

Wolfe Tone arrived at Philadelphia on 1st August 1795. At once he approached the French Ambassador. But his reception was so chilly that he concluded that nothing could be done, and began arrangements for making a living in the United States, which displeased him but could not be avoided.

It may be that the course of events in France decided the Ambassador not to court trouble. The year following the rising of August 1792 saw the French Revolution at its meridian. The revolutionary democracy, typified by the Commune, was necessary to defend the Republic. But its two public leaders, Danton and Robespierre, who together bestrode the stage, represented two forms of one alternative to the "war of liberation" desired by the masses. The alternative was to split the coalition against France, Danton seeking peace with England to be free to fight Germany, Robespierre seeking the settlement with the German powers. The success of Pitt in shutting out Fox and the Whig peace party from all influence in the government made Danton's position untenable. The terror was then "intensified to a pitch of insanity, because it was necessary to keep Robespierre in power under the existing internal conditions.''[51]

But when the French victory at Fleurus gave France command of the left bank of the Rhine on 24th June 1794, the military danger was over, and the underlying cause of the terror removed. Robespierre fell next month. The war continued, objectively rooting out social anachronisms that were worthy of destruction, objectively preserving a society that had taken a step forward from powers anxious to drag it back, but it was no longer the consciously intended war of liberation. In France the return of security brought the return of "normality," that is to say of Government roughly corresponding to the real balance of class forces. Within this balance the upper stratum of the bourgeoisie steadily strengthened its position with the support of the emancipated peasantry.

This process reflected itself in endless struggles within the revolutionary Government, while French Generals were winning spectacular victories in central Europe, and Carnot was earning his title of "the organiser of victory" who turned the raw recruits of the mass levy into the most formidable army Europe had ever seen. When Tone approached the Ambassador the Convention had been in uproar for months; in October it handed over its powers to a Directory composed of Barras, Carnot, La Reveillere, Letourneur and Rewbell. By the end of the year French policy was again clear. It was to continue the war against England. Ambassadors could breathe freely again.

In November Tone received letters from Keogh, Russell and the Simmses telling him the result of the Government offensive, and saying that "the state of the public mind in Ireland was advancing to Republicanism faster than even I could believe." They pressed him to hasten the common plan of action. When he approached the French ambassador once more, he found him entirely co-operative. Letters of introduction were provided. After sending his young brother to inform his friends in Ireland, he left for France on January 1st, 1796.

Once in Paris he conferred with the American Ambassador, and sought out the French Foreign Minister De la Croix. He was at once referred to his under-secretary Madgett. From him he received plenty of encouragment but no satisfaction. His irritations are recorded in his journals which give a striking and intimate picture of French life at this period. At last, exasperated by talk and procrastination, he returned to Monroe who advised him to drop "the subaltern way of doing things" and to deal only with principals. He took the advice, and on 24th

February with much trepidation went to the Luxembourg to demand an interview with Carnot.

Carnot saw him. Two days later De la Croix assured him that the policy of the Directory was to effect the separation of Ireland from England and to establish her as an independent Republic in alliance with France. By llth March Tone had come to the conclusion that if there was to be any change of Government in France, "I should be glad if the Jacobins were to come again into play, for I think a little more energy just now would do the French Government no harm." There were long discussions with De la Croix over the size of the force required, and the amount of support it would have in Ireland. "Requisition! Requisitionl!" wrote Tone. "Our independence must be had at all hazards. If the men of property will not support us, they must fall; we can support ourselves by the aid of the numerous and respectable class the men of no property."*

Nothing having happened in three weeks, Tone approached Carnot again on March 14th and this time was put in touch with General Clarke who asked him if the aristocracy would support the invasion. "Most certainly not," said Tone, and "begged him to remember if the attempt were made it would be by the people and the people only." How would it end, asked Clarke. "In a Republic allied to France." But would the Catholic clergy not forbid it? Tone recorded his reply:-

> *"Within these last few years, that is to say since the French Revolution, an astonishing change with regard to the influence of the priests had taken place in Ireland. . . I mentioned the circumstance of the clergy excommunicating all Defenders and even refusing the sacraments to some of the poor fellows in articulo mortis, which to a Catholic is a very serious affair, and all to no purpose."*

INDECISION

Of Madgett's exasperating sloth Tone wrote: "I do not understand people being idle and giving themselves airs, and wanting to make revolutions, whilst they are grumbling at the trouble of writing a few sheets of paper." Irritation mounted as delay seemed to succeed delay.

---

*The phrase "numerous and respectable" is a jocular allusion to the habit in eighteenth-century newspapers of reporting every gathering of the Whigs and merchants as "numerous and respectable"

Disquieting news came from Ireland, and Tone "wished to God" he had — the cliche had to his ears the ring of "a good time was had by all." Rusell or Keogh were with him. He spent his time writing, planning or merely sightseeing. He had been in theory a "martinet" in military discipline; examination of the French army at close quarters convinced him that the most important quality was revolutionary enthusiasm." If we go on in Ireland, we must move heaven and earth to create the same spirit of enthusiasm which I see here." This could, of course, only come as a result of returning the land to the people, a policy Tone edged nearer to the following year. Struck as he was with the sartorial latitude of the French army, he went to the Council of five-hundred and received the same impression. Their appearance was extremely plain. They reminded him of the Catholic committee, but the Committee "looked more like gentlemen." Then reflecting that of all the deliberative assemblies he had seen that in Dublin was incomparably the worst, he adds of the French, "It is very little matter what they look like. They have humbled Europe thus far . . . the rest is of little consequence." Even while awaiting a definite decision for action Tone had to be continually dissuading the French from foolish proposals which came from sources which were, he thought, unreliable. He was strongly opposed to sending prisoners to Ireland. "If these ragamuffins are smuggled into the country, local insurrections will ensue, the militia will obey their officials, the bravest of our poor peasants will be cut down." He wanted a strong force equipped with ample armament to land at Sligo and make for Belfast. At the same time he made it clear that the French force must be subordinate to the Irish provisional military Government. "I for one will never be accessory to subjecting my country to the control of France merely to get rid of England."

ACTION AT LAST
In May he called on Carnot for the third time and left thinking he was back where he started. But on June 23rd he was told by General Clarke that the invasion had been agreed in principle, even to the date, and that the only question now was the manner. What had happened was that seeing the Indemnity and Insurrection Acts left them no constitutional openings whatever, the Executive of the United Irishmen called an emergency meeting in May 1796. O'Connor was already abroad at the time and Lord Edward Fitzgerald was sent to accompany him to Switzerland where they met General Hoche in June. The general

agreement communicated to Tone was particularised in August, and immediately afterwards the United Irishmen became a military organisation. This involved little alteration of their organisation as a secret society. Military titles, military methods were "engrafted" on the civil; arms were collected, and pikes forged in expectation of the arrival of the French. On July 12th, Tone met Hoche, who, it was agreed, was to lead the expedition. Hoche had Jacobin sympathies. Was there any danger, he asked, of the Catholics setting up a Monarchy? What Tone by now called the "old arguments" were gone over again.

"I summed up all," he wrote, *"by telling them that as to religion my belief was we should content ourselves with pulling down the establishment without setting up any other; that we should have no state religion but let every sect* pay their own clergy voluntarily; that as to royalty and aristocracy, they were both odious in Ireland to that degree that I apprehended much more a general massacre of the gentry and the distribution of the entire of their property, than the establishment of any form of government which would perpetuate their influence; that I hoped this massacre would not happen and that I for one would do all that lay in my power to prevent it, because I did not like blood, even of the guilty; at the same time that the pride, cruelty and oppression of the Irish aristocracy were so great that I apprehended every excess from the just resentment of the people."*

Many have rightly admired this fine statement of revolutionary principles, repudiating atrocities but placing the responsibility for the excesses of the people upon their oppressors. It has not usually been pointed out, however, that while Tone promised to do his utmost to avoid the massacre, he engaged in no undertaking to try to prevent "the distribution of the entire of their property." The guilty class was named and the popular remedy was broached.

BANTRY BAY

Tone and Hoche soon became fast friends, and their mutual respect steadily increased. Tone was given a commission in the French Army,

---

*Those who have jibbed at the word think it is derived from *secare* (to cut). It is not. Like sept it comes from *sequi* (to follow) and Tone meant a following, not a break-away.

and was constantly in the General's entourage. Hoche was at this time a man of thirty-two years. Tone found some of his assistants less forthcoming:-

> *"I always find the subalterns greater men than the principals. One thing I must keep in mind. As I have begun by dancing attendance on others, if ever I arrive at any situation, I must remember the anxiety and vexation I suffered in my time, and not give myself airs."*

After seemingly interminable delays he arrived at Rennes, the old capital of Brittany, on September 20th. Delays continued. It seemed as if the navy was determined to prevent the expedition. On October 22nd, they set out for Brest. A week later news arrived that Russell and Neilson had been arrested for high treason. Tone was filled with rage and desperation at the news. A young man arrived from Ireland saying that the country was in a ferment waiting for the French. In mid-November Hoche told him that Villaret Joyeuse, the admiral, had been cashiered for his dilatoriness. Things promised to speed up. But next week Hoche himself fell ill. At last, on December 16th, the expedition sailed from Brest harbour. It consisted of 17 ships of the line, 13 frigates, 7 corvettes, and 6 transports — 43 sail. On board were 15,000 soldiers, mostly veterans of the Vendée, 41,000 stand of arms, 29 pieces of artillery, 61,000 barrels of gunpowder, and 7,000,000 ball cartridges. Had such an armament landed in Ulster, Ireland would have been separated from Britain. Tone had strongly urged a landing in the north, but was overruled. This had no effect on the success of the expedition, which met with an almost incredible succession of accidents. Hoche had contrived to feed the British intelligence system the erroneous notion that an attack was intended on Portugal. The Channel was thus clear of the British navy. But immediately after leaving Brest the French ships became separated. The Fraternite, carrying Hoche, was missing. The agreed rendezvous in case of a separation (not the proposed point of landing) was Bantry Bay. In a fair wind and with Grouchy in command, the thirty-five sail which had effected a re-junction, reached the appointed place. The orders were to cruise five days.

> *"There cannot be imagined,"* wrote Tone, *"a situation more provokingly tantalising than mine at this moment; within view, almost within reach of my native land, and uncertain I shall ever*

set foot on it. We are now (nine o'clock December 21st) at the rendezvous appointed; stood in for the coast till twelve, when we were near enough to toss a biscuit ashore; at twelve tacked and stood out again; so now we have begun our cruise of five days in all its forms, and shall, in obedience to the letter of our instructions, ruin the expedition, and destroy the remnant of the French Navy, with a precision and a punctuality which will be truly edifying. We opened Bantry Bay, and in all my life rage never entered so deeply into my heart as when we turned our backs on the coast.''

After three days, while the West Cork tenants were obediently lugging British artillery up the snowy mountain tracks in hopes of meeting the invasion, and sharing their potatoes with the troops, Grouchy agreed to land 6,500 men without tent, or horse, or money that is to say merely with arms and clothing. The plan was to march rapidly on Cork City. One and a half hours would have been sufficient for the landing. But almost the hour the decision was made, an easterly gale sprang up which increased to a hurricane. After some debate over sailing north seeking the separated ships, it was decided to return to Brest. So ended the greatest naval force to threaten Britain since the Spanish Armada. The attempt to relieve the beleaguered democracy of Ireland had failed, and the gruesome horror of the next year became inevitable.

6

The Terror

The failure of the Bantry Bay expedition caused deep disappointment in Ireland. Worse perhaps than the revelation of French indecisiveness and the weakness of the United Irishmen in the south, was the frustration that arises from unforseeable sheer bad luck. Even in the north some of the propertied elements began to waver and rumours spread that the Catholic Committee was prepared to attempt a separate settlement with the Government.

In order to hold the movement together and check possible reprisals by the Government, O'Connor and Emmet made proposals for conciliation. Would a Government frightened by the imminence of French invasion be prepared to forestall a second attempt by granting substantial concessions, thus reversing the process by which authority was degenerating into terror? On 2nd January 1797 a public meeting was held in Belfast at which a resolution was passed stating that the imperfect state of representation in the House of Commons was the primary cause of discontent in the country, and that a reform of Parliament would secure tranquility providing it secured to population and property their due weight in the scale of government. This would "conciliate the affections of the people, whose object is reform alone, and thereby constitute the only rampart of defence that can bid defiance to the efforts of foreign and domestic enemies." The resolution offered to accept a Government of King, Lords and Commons "wisely and honestly administered." Efforts were made to secure the co-operation of the Whigs.

The initiative came to nothing — as it could only come to nothing. It was an effort to restore the position of 1779-82 in totally changed conditions. The restoration of democracy, at a time when Ulster alone contained 100,000 United Irishmen, would have meant revolution. O'Connor and Emmet could be as conciliatory as they wished. They knew, and the Government knew, that for it to ease the terror was to be engulfed. The Irish administration was already the prisoner of its past actions. The consolidation of the Irish nation required the liquidation of the great landlords as a class. The relaxation of their dictatorship would simply clear the way for it. At the same time the forces gathered against them in preparation for a terrible confrontation Their necessities drove them forward to fresh follies and created for them fresh dfficulties. It is in this sense that the British Government in effecting the Union "rescued" the aristocracy of Ireland from destruction — but at the same time "took prisoner" the merchant and industrial classes.

PRESS SUPPRESSED

The decision of the Government followed logically from its class character. It was to intensify the terror against the people, and disarm the revolutionaries. Its first aim was to destroy their great educator and rallying point, the *Northern Star*. The importance of this can best be judged against the general state of the press in Ireland at this time. Mr Brian Inglis[52] had divided it into four categories, Castle, commercial, opposition and revolutionary. The first category included the *Freeman's Journal, Faulkner's Dublin Journal, Hibernian Telegraph* and *General Evening Post*. The *Freeman's Journal* was edited by the arch-informer and mountebank Francis Higgins, the "Sham Squire;"[53] Faulkner's by an informer equally notorious, John Giffard, the "Dog-in-Office." Corbet, editor of the *Telegraph*, "combined his newspaper work with activities as a government agent, especially in their dealings with journalists." Carey of the *Post* was a former democrat whose financial difficulties led him to sell himself to the administration.

The brazenness of these newspapers is only paralleled by the enormous sums put at their editors' disposal by the Government. The commercial press was effectively muzzled by the use of "fiats" (large sums of bail against possible misdemeanours) and a liberal intepretation of the law of libel. The opposition papers of Whig tendency clung to a precarious existence until mid-1798 when the last of them (the *Cork Gazette*) folded up under political and financial pressure. Their moderation and circumspection did not save them. The only effective opposition was therefore the *Northern Star*. Already in September 1796, the informer Bird, "a spy whose duplicity bordered on insanity," had sworn information which led to the arrest of Samuel Neilson who was held without charge or trial. The paper struggled on till February 3rd when Colonel Barber raided the premises and seized the printing equipment. In this raid the Simms brothers were arrested. The paper nevertheless reappeared on February 24th, but with inferior machinery and inexperienced staff. Its effectiveness was correspondingly diminished, but it was not finally extinguished until 19th May 1797, after the editor had refused to insert a statement by the Monaghan yeomanry offensive to the people of Belfast — not, as is asserted in the *History of Orangeism*, after inserting a paragraph offensive to that regiment. A number of the soldiers marched from their barracks at North Queen Street, smashed the formes and "threw everything they could find into Wilson's entry," seizing some of the workmen while others escaped through a back exit."[50] Undoubtedly the suppression of the *Northern Star* seriously disarrayed the organisation in the north.

CALL TO REVOLT

The United Irishmen were without a journal until the following September when with rare courage a youth named Finnerty agreed to the use of his name as printer of a newspaper launched by Arthur O'Connor in Dublin. *The Dublin Press*,[54] as it was called, was a most striking production, to be compared in ways with the famous *Workers' Republic* James Connolly edited and printed behind an armed guard at Liberty Hall a century later. It announced itself the successor of the *Northern Star*, but struck a more vigorous note from the start, demanding the restoration of the full liberty of the press, condemning the outrages of the Orange militia and yeomanry. From its pages it is possible to glean some account of the terror in Belfast. The affairs of the United Irishmen were discussed in Montanus's articles, *"Letters from the mountains"* — a double meaning since the "mountain" in France signified the Jacobins from their position in the assembly, and also the preparations for revolt going on in the hills.

The call to revolt grew clearer every day — "the day must come when the people shall firmly rally around the constitution and range themselves boldly under tbe standard of freedom." But Montanus consistently warned against premature action and yielding to provocation. "The day comes when justice shall prevail, when Ireland shall raise her head from the dust and perform a solemn sacrifice to the constitution." The code-word was obviously "constitution," clearly understood since the constitution had been subverted by the Government.

Finnerty was arrested in December and defended by Curran. O'Connor then announced himself proprietor and struggled on for two months. The last extant edition contains an address of the London Corresponding Society to the Irish nation, a proof of the fact that at all times the common interest of the democracies of the two countries was understood.

The winter of 1797 was the highest point of organisation of the United Irishmen in Ulster. The administration had produced the very effect it most feared. Instead of converting Catholics into Defenders and cutting them off a few at a time, it had forced them into the arms of the "United Irishmen." Defenderism all but disappeared. Dictatorship repeatedly found its weapons breaking in its hand. The Militia had been embodied to replace the Volunteers. Now these in turn began to show signs of unreliability. A yeomanry was recruited after the English model and filled with members of the Orange bands. But these were insufficient. Fencible regiments were then brought from Scotland, and a band of mounted riff-raff miscalled the "Ancient Britons," commanded by Sir Watkin Williams-Wynn, a member of an Anglo-Welsh Jacobite family grown wealthy on the seizure of the common lands of North Wales, and growing wealthier still on the labour of the miners of Flint and Denbigh.[55] While quietly dissociating itself from the policies of the Dublin Government, the British Government had no objection to providing it with the means of enforcing them.

PITCHCAPS

In March the Government decided it was now or never. On the 3rd, Secretary Pelham wrote to General Lake, commander of the forces in Ulster, directing him to disarm the province. He must "suppress all outrage," and "disperse all assemblies having a tendency to outrage, without waiting for the civil authority." This was a declaration of war on the people of Ulster.

The General was not disobliging. On March 13th he announced his intention of acting "in such a manner as the public safety required" and invited all who had knowledge of concealed arms or ammunition to offer information under guarantee of immunity and promise of reward. Now there was organised the legion of spies and provocateurs known as the "Battalion of testimony". Treachery and perjury became their stock in trade. Recruited from the dregs of the population, the informers were given a special training by the authorities and power and opportunities they could never have dreamed of. It was at this period that there commenced the practice of torturing to extract confessions.

During the house-to-house searches for arms which ensued there was a steady crescendo of atrocity. Militia objected to the work and had to be confined to the towns.* Regiments from England, where mutinies were already taking place both in army and navy, proved unreliable and one had to be hastily bundled back to England. Only Sir Watkin Wynn's version of the "Black-and-Tans" and the armed Orange mobs which formed the yeomanry could he relied on for certain, and it was these who carried out the "domiciliary visits," tortured without respect for age or sex and left smoking ruins throughout the fertile land of Ulster. At first their favourite torture was flogging — up to 500 lashes being inflicted, some victims committing suicide to escape it. Tiring of the monotony of this pastime they introduced "picketing" — a variety of crucifixion in which the victim was fastened, back to the ground, his wrists and ankles drawn to full stretch by cords tied to picket pegs. Then followed the roasting of the victim's feet at his own turf fire and the amiable practice of "half-hanging." Finally came the pitch-cap — a piece of strong linen or brown paper saturated with molten pitch which was fixed on to the head of the victim who was not only tortured by the heat but blinded by the liquid pitch running into his eyes. An improvement on the pitch-cap for those who liked quick work was the gunpowder cap; moistened gunpowder was rubbed into the scalp, which was then fired.**

The repressive measures of the Government placed the United Irishmen in a dilemma, whether to strike now and lose the opportunity of French aid, or to wait for the French at the possible expense of their power to support them. In parts of Ulster, notably Co. Down, the United Irishmen resisted attempts to disarm them. The Dublin leadership was, however, playing for time and there were some exchanges on the subiect of the follies of prematurity and the perils of delay.

---

*The Dublin Press contained a letter professedly by a militia officer which states that "the native troops of Ireland will never turn their arms against their country or home."
**Every vestige of hair was burned off and the skin raised in sores and blisters. Lord Clare justified these barbarities by arguing that "he thought example necessary" and that "there were certain cases which justified severity, and in which it became mercy; and he would submit whether the consequences provided against might not have been more terrible than the sufferings of the traitors."

SECOND ATTEMPT

Tone, biding impatiently in France, inclined to the view of the Ulstermen, on the probable grounds that action in Ireland would accelerate a second French invasion. During several months of waiting, he left Paris to meet his wife and family who had landed in Germany. On his return he met Lewines who had been sent by the United Irishmen to press for a second invasion. Hoche went to Paris personally to urge it. In the result the French included the liberation of Ireland in their war aims, and it was agreed that the next attempt would be the responsibility of the Dutch, who were willing to hazard their last ship and their last shilling to make themselves a power in Europe once again.

During the preparations, Van Leyden observed to Tone that judging by his own visit to Ireland, where he observed the extreme contrast between the luxury of the rich and the misery of the poor, "no country in Europe had so crying a need for the revolution." Tone replied that "one great motive of our conduct in this business was the conviction of the wretched state of our peasantry and the determination, if possible, to amend it."

In July all was ready. All that was required was a fair wind. But from 17th July until September lst the wind blew steadily from the southwest, except for a few hours. The fleet was bottled up in the Texel during the vital period when the British Navy was disorganised by mutiny and its aftermath. Teeling and MacNeven took back to Ireland the promise of an expedition that never came. For, following its postponement, the Dutch fleet sallied forth, only to be annihilated by the British on October 11th at Camperdown.

During 1797 the tide of revolution began to ebb fast. While learning daily of the arrest of his friends at home, Tone observed around him a steady cooling of temper, a slipping away from the high principles the revolution was reputed to stand for. Intrigues were set afoot against Grouchy on his return from Bantry Bay. The Royalists stepped up their attacks on the Directory and prompted Tone's comment that "The liberty of the press is not yet understood in France; the indecent attacks which are made with impunity on the Government are scandalous and abominable . . . 'liberty of the press' is like liberty to carry a stick." The attacks increased to such a point that there was talk of overthrowing the Directory. Hoche told Tone that in the event of such an attempt he would march his army on Paris to preserve the constitution. Convinced of his Jacobin sympathies the royalists then turned their attention to Hoche, who was mortified to such measure that Tone marvelled that a man so brave before cannon should be so vulnerable to words. A rival appeared in the young Buonaparte, whose arrogant declaration to the Government of Genoa alarmed Tone and led him to warn Hoche aginst attempting anything similar in Ireland. The issue between the two generals was never fought out. Hoche had been suffering from tuberculosis for some time. The disease advanced rapidly during the summer and on September 18th he died. It was Buonaparte whose general Augereau seized the Tuileries and expelled Carnot. On October 16th, still asserting that they would "never quit England until the independence of Ireland should be recognised" the Directory announced the establishment of the "Army of England" with Buonaparte in command. In December the Directory told Lewines that the third attempt to invade England would be in April 1798.

HOPE DEFERRED
The effect in Ireland of the constant expectation and repeated delay was disastrous. Throughout 1797 the persecution continued. The leaders of the United Irishmen must maintain their organisation, preserve their arms, drill their men, but impose the almost intolerable discipline of holding fire until the French came. During the summer attempts were made to repair the weakness of the organisation in Munster. The missionaries sent to the south received a ready hearing. The members of the old agrarian defence societies came over to the United Irishmen in large numbers, further emphasising the class character of the struggle.

Under Lord Carhampton the army and yeomanry became little better than a banditry. It was remarked however that the Government obstructed measures that were standard military practice while tolerating irregularities and provocations. His army became "formidable to everyone but the enemy," and he resigned in protest. His successor, Lord Abercromby, endeavoured to restore discipline without avail. The type of assistance he could expect from the administration was illustrated by Lord Clare's reply to a question in Parliament relating to a case of half-hanging. "Nothing more was done," Fitzgibbon explained, "than tying a rope about the man's neck to induce him to confess." Abercromby resigned and General Lake took his place. The correct balance was thus achieved — oppression arbitrary enough to provoke resistance, and undisciplined enough for the most savage repression.

That the administration was taking deliberate measures to secure that a revolt would "explode" was admitted by the Secret Committee in its subsequent enquiry. During the latter part of 1797 the strength of the United Irishmen began to fail in the north, notwithstanding the execution of William Orr on the charge of administering the "United" oath to a soldier. Members of the jury admitted being drunk during their deliberations and the soldier himself retracted his testimony. Indignation reached fever pitch and to all United Irishmen the words "remember Orr" were a challenge to reaffirm their faith.

But though numbers remained the same on paper determination faltered. To some extent this was due to the hesitations of the merchant class who were doing well out of the war, despite the financial crisis in which it involved the British Government. The disarming of Ulster, though by no means complete, combined with the sense of disappointment both in the French and in the people of the south to induce a mood of caution in the hard-headed northerners. Half-promises of Catholic emancipation after "Jacobinism" had been crushed were snapped at by the hierarchy , and the old cordiality between Catholics and Dissenters, though not broken, began to sink to a more passive level.

Underlying all and perhaps grasped instinctively by the Jacobins of Ulster, was the ending of the revolutionary period in France, and the beginning of the process which led through the Empire to the restoration and the establishment of the great European prison house with its three chief jailors, Britain, Austria and Russia, on the walls of which repeated revolutions battered themselves in vain until 1917. The consequence was that the Catholics first, then the Dissenters, began to publish loyal addresses to King and Constitution.[29] This could only mean that despairing of the French establishing a democratic constitution, their hopes were being transferred to Britain. This fact should be remembered in view of Catholic support for the Union.

BUONAPARTE'S BETRAYAL

At the end of 1797 Wolfe Tone met Buonaparte and urged the use of the army of England in Ireland. He received no firm assurance. Buonaparte had secured his predominance by a demagogical appeal to Jacobin sentiment. But the Directory had its suspicions of his ultimate intentions, whence a disinclination to afford him the opportunity of covering himself with glory too near to France.

97

Meanwhile Paris began to fill with refugees, mostly Irish, but some English and Scottish who had fled from the "carnival of reaction" established by Pitt in the United Kingdom. As often occurs with refugees whose real place in the world has become untenable, factions, intrigues and fantasies often took the place of practical political work. Tone had his work cut out with some of the newly arrived generalissimos whose jealousy of his own established position was equalled only by their impatience to assume it.

He could afford to laugh at Paine's absurd egoism and his new-fangled pantheistic religion. Thomas Muir he dismissed as an "arrogant blockead." But Tandy's strutting and parading as a "general" of the United Irishmen, together with much other puerility, was of some consequence as weakening French confidence in the seriousness of the Irish. These men were, of course, unconsciously expressing their frustration at the sickening of their great cause. As modesty is typical of the revolutionary in action, so arrogance is the characteristic cloak of unacknowledged defeat. When in April 1798 Tone learned that Buonaparte was taking the Army of England to Egypt, all seemed lost.

News of Arthur O'Connor's arrest at Margate came in mid-March. Events in Ireland had begun to move fast. Rumours of a rising in Ireland grew stronger, and Tone hoped that here was no partial affair, as he redoubled his efforts to secure French action. Although unaware of the degree to which Ulster had fallen off, Tone fully appreciated the class basis of the impending struggle and in his journal of 26 April made one of his clearest pronouncements:-

> *"What miserable slaves are the gentry of Ireland. The only accusation brought against the United Irishmen by their enemies is that they wish to break the connection with England. . . but it will be said that the United Irishmen extend their views further; they go now for a distribution of property and an agrarian law. I know not whether they do so now. I am sure in June 1795 when I was forced to leave the country, they entertained no such ideas. If they have since taken root among them, the Irish gentry may accuse themselves. . . if such men in the issue lose their property, they are themselves to blame . . . They see Ireland only in their rent-rolls, their places, their patronage and their pensions. They shall perish like their own dung. Those who have seen them shall say 'where are they?' "*

It is sometimes stated that the United Irishmen's organisation was so riddled with spies and informers that its leaders could scarcely cough without the fact being known to the Castle. This is an exaggeration. The Castle had erected an enormous organisation for provocation and above all false witness, but the betrayal of the plans of the Union was the work of one or two well-placed provocateurs, which indeed was all that was necessary. The most notorious of these, the informer Reynolds, discovering that the Leinster Directory was to meet at the house of Oliver Bond on March 12th, informed the Castle, with the result that the entire Directory was arrested, save only Lord Edward Fitzgerald who went into hiding. The leadership was taken over by the brothers Sheares, of one of whom, the leader, Jonah Barrington wrote that "he was well-educated but mistook the phrases of republicanism for a power of writing in its defence, and of being a leader in its cause." This dictum on a sincere and uncompromising revolutionist was fair. At that time, when the whole policy of government might be summed up in the one word provocation, a cool head and a realistic temper were above all required. Tone spoke similarly of Stokes, "I fear very much that his very metaphysical and unbending purity, which can accommodate itself neither to men, times nor circumstances, will always prevent his being of any service to his country." Such was the character of the "middle leadership" now thrust into control. This situation the government now used to its advantage. As late as March 25th the Ulster Directory was assured that the French would begin embarkation early in April. A week later a message to the same effect reached Leinster. But on March 30th the Government struck decisively. A proclamation was issued by the Lord Lieutenant and Council declaring the country in a state of rebellion. The army was enjoined to employ itself "with the utmost vigour and decision for the immediate suppression thereof, and also to recover the arms which have been traitorously forced from his Majesty's peaceable and loyal subjects, and to disarm the rebels, and all persons disaffected to his Majesty's Government, by the most summary and effectual measures . . ." The proclamation was followed by an announcement in many counties that unless all arms and ammunition were given up within ten days, "the troops should be quartered in large bodies to live at free quarters among them and other very severe means would be used to enforce obedience." As the Secret Committee agreed, "the leaders found themselves reduced to the alternative of immediate insurrection, or of being deprived of the means on which they relied for effecting that purpose."

THE RISING

The effect of the Government proclamation was electric. At once "from the humble cot to the stately mansion, no property, no person was secure." Hundreds perished under the lash. Many were strangled in efforts to extort confessions. The picket and the pitch-cap did double duty in the hands of the armed torturers. One unfortunate who was smeared from head to foot with turpentine and pitch rushed flaming from the Old Custom House and plunged to his death in the Liffey. In Drogheda a man was flogged to death at the cart-tail for wearing a small ring bearing a shamrock insignia. The people were goaded beyond all endurance and the Leinstermen had no choice but to strike. May 23rd was the chosen date. Four days before it, the Sham Squire earned £1,000 for detecting and delivering up Lord Edward Fitzgerald. On the 21st the brothers Sheares were arrested, thanks to a Militia Captain they had mistakenly trusted. But the insurrection began. It was the work of the common people.

The rising of May 23rd 1798 is in a sense the "first general uprising of the Irish working class." It is most notable that the day began with what can only be adequately described as a general strike. According to Plowden, "It is a most melancholy proof of the progress of rebellion that every person, almost without distinction, in and about Dublin, whose situation in life put him in the occasion of retaining any number of men, either as servants, artificers, workmen or labourers, was suddenly left and abandoned by those persons attending their respective posts for the general rising." The confusion was indescribable since at dusk it was found that the lamplighters had struck as a body and the city was in darkness. The signal for the rising was to be the stopping of the mail coaches. Risings took place in the counties of Dublin, Kildare and Wicklow, and at more distant points when the coaches failed to appear. The rebels were unable, however, to carry through their plans of an assault on the city, and the Government was thus enabled to regain the initiative and enforce martial law throughout the whole country. The armed forces were ordered to put down the rebellion "according to martial law, either by death or otherwise."

The significance of the word "otherwise" has already been indicated.

100

A curfew was imposed. Citizens were compelled to place lists on their doorposts of all who resided within. Military executions began and soon the bridges and lampirons of Dublin were decorated with the corpses of those who had not been given the slightest formality of a trial.

Whether the organisation of the United Irishmen could have survived the shattering of their plans for insurrection is debateable. There is no doubt, however, that Government policy was to goad every part of Ireland where they existed in any strength into a rebellion that they could crush by the most sanguinary means. Thanks to the accident that their representatives had not reached the Leinster Directory when it was dispersed the United organisation in Wexford was still intact. The atrocities of April and May led to an extremely rapid enrolment among a people not previously subjected to severe repression. The strongest resistance therefore occurred in this comparatively prosperous county, a corner of Ireland of extreme beauty and fertility bounded on the west by high mountains and on the south and east by the sea.

WEXFORD

The story of the Wexford Rising has been told many times, most recently by Mr. Dickson,[56] and would require more space than is available here. Suffice to say that in April 1798 the North Cork militia imported into the county its full paraphernalia of repression with pitchcaps, pickets and cat o'nine tails embellished with orange ribbons. Any person found with his hair cut short was likely to be a victim of their attentions. Women were exposed to gross insults, their clothing being searched for garments bearing any item coloured green. Men's ears and noses were cut off. Free quarters became a riot of robbery and atrocity. The result was that the people fled from their homes and slept in fields and ditches, which immediately became recruiting grounds for the United Irishmen. The rising flared up when Father Murphy of Boolavogue, seeing his church in flames and appealed to by his homeless parishioners, decided to put himself at the head of an armed force, on the grounds that death would come anyway and therefore it was best to die resisting.

The Wexford Rising makes one of the most glorious chapters in Irish history. The resistance movement spread rapidly and reached its height in the neighbourhood of Gorey, where the United Irishmen had been longest established. In one encounter, at Arklow, the insurgents so far overcame their enemies that did they but know it, they could have marched on Dublin. Their example spread into the neighbouring counties of Carlow and Wicklow, and it was many months before the Government could put down the guerillas in the mountains. For some time Wexford Town was in the hands of the insurgents, who conducted their affairs with a moderation in sharp contrast to that of the Government troops. They set their face firmly against reprisals and sectarianism, and concluded their proclamation with the words, "God save the people." That there were some spontaneous reprisals goes without saying. Men are but human and it could not be expected that those who had the opportunity to break even with those who had pitch-capped, whipped and half-strangled them would always resist the temptation to make full avail of it. The rising was not crushed until the end of June, when the bloody reprisals of the authorities made all rebel excesses pale into insignificance. General Sir John Moore, who accepted the surrender of Wexford, remarked confidentially to Grattan, "If I were an Irishman I would be a rebel." While the Wexford struggle was in progress a last attempt was made in Ulster. Henry Joy McCracken led a rising in Antrim in the "First year of Liberty" on 6th June 1798. But the old spirit of Ulster was no more. Within three days it was defeated and McCracken a prisoner. On June 9th Co. Down rose. Despite much brave resistance, the struggle was over by the 13th. Antrim and Ballynahinch could do nothing without Belfast. And Belfast had been crushed. There was also a small rising in West Cork. But neither Leinster nor Ulster could prove succesful without the French. The progress of two decades since 1779 had led to such a monstrous proliferation of corruption in society at large, that once the top leadership of the United Irishmen were arrested and dispersed, there could be no coordinating force except one from abroad. The oligarchy which controlled the independent legislature had destroyed the popular sanction it rested on, and made foreign intervention an inevitability. When this came it was in the form of the Union.

LAST EFFORT

The news from Ireland once more stirred French interest. Buonaparte had left Toulon on May 20, three days before the insurrection his dream of personal glory had betrayed. Without waiting for proper orders, the gallant soldier of fortune, General Humbert, "whose heart was better than his head," decided to begin the invasion on his own. He would thus compel the Directory either to second or to disown him. He made the coast of Connaught on 22nd August, and landed at Killala, thus drawing into the struggle the fourth and last province of Ireland. Tone's son considered that his wisest plan would have been to push at once to Ulster, where the arrival of a strong force might still have stirred the embers into a blaze. Be that as it may, Humbert spent two weeks drilling the peasants and organising a kind of local republic. After scoring some brilliant military successes at Castlebar and as far east as the Co. Longford, he was ultimately defeated and taken prisoner. The Directory decided to support him, and sent Hardy with 3,000 men on September 14th. On September 16th Tandy and his associates left in a small boat, landed on Rathlin, learned of Humbert's defeat, and after distributing some proclamations, escaped to Norway. Wolfe Tone, who had stated his willingness to land in Ireland with a corporal's guard, accompanied Hardy and is said to have exposed himself fearlessly during the naval battle off the Donegal coast on October 12th.

The French Fleet was defeated and Tone and his fellow officers taken prisoner. Tone was recognised, and despite his status as a French officer, put in irons and conveyed to Dublin. He was held in jail under the notorious Major Sandys, whose "insolence, rapacity and cruelty will long be remembered in that city where, a worthy instrument of the faction which then ruled it, he enjoyed, with their patronage, a despotic authority within its precincts." He was tried by a court-martial on November 10th. His speech from the dock has passed into history. "From my earliest youth," he declared, "I have regarded the connection between Ireland and Great Britain as the curse of the Irish nation: and I felt convinced that whilst it lasted this country could never be free nor happy. My mind has been confirmed in this opinion by every succeeding year, and the conclusion which I have drawn from every fact before my eyes. In consequence, I determined to apply all the powers which my individual efforts could move in order to separate the two countries." Tone was not permitted to read a passage in which he thanked the Catholics for their loyalty to him in 1794. He was found guilty of treason and sentenced to death.

Two things should be noted about this trial. First, as Tone wrote to the French Directory, he was a French citizen and held a commission in the French army. The court refused to recognise this status. Second, the court-martial itself was completely illegal, since the civil courts were sitting. It was on this ground that the great people's advocate, John Philpot Curran, moved for a writ of *habeas corpus* on the grounds of

103

illegal detention. The application was made on November 12th, Tone's father making the necessary affidavit, that his son had been brought before a bench of military officers calling themselves a court-martial and had been by them illegally sentenced to death. The Lord Chief Justice, the humane Lord Kilwarden, ordered a writ to be instantly prepared. My client may die while this writ is preparing," Curran rejoined. "Proceed to the barracks," Kilwarden told the Sheriff, "and acquaint the provost marshal that a writ is preparing to suspend Mr Tone's execution; and see that he be not executed." The Sheriff returned with the news that the Provost Marshal replied that he must obey Major Sandys, and Major Sandys that he must obey Lord Cornwallis. Immediately afterwards Peter Tone returned with the news that General Craig in whose custody Tone was, had seen the writ of habeas corpus and had refused to obey it. Kilwarden then ordered the arrest of the Provost Marshal, and Major Sandys, and that General Craig be shown the order of the court to this effect. Curran and his friends believed that if Tone could be brought before the civil court the delay involved might give the Directory time to exchange him against some notable British prisoner, and it is stated that steps in this direction were already being taken. When the Sheriff returned it was with the news that "Mr. Tone having cut his throat the night before, was not in a condition to be moved." A French emigre surgeon testified to having attended Tone at four of the preceding night. The Chief Justice then made an order suspending the execution of Tone which was to be served at once on the proper persons. Tone did not require it. He lingered for a few days and expired on November 19th.

DEATH OF TONE
The circumstances of his death at once suggested that, realising that the bringing of the case into a civil court might lead to the escape of the most dangerous man in Ireland, who might plague British imperialism for a full forty years yet, his captors decided to do away with him. On this subject his son drew attention to the suspicious circumstance that no visitors were permitted to see him and no post mortem was allowed. "The character of the man, the seclusion in which the prisoner was kept; no medical attendant was even allowed to see him except the emigrant French surgeon . . . would justify almost any suspicion." His son decided the balance against murder on the basis of statements made by Tone some time previously, which do not however show any clear

104

intention of suicide in the event of capture.

On this subject Frank McDermot says "that he cut his throat is, in fact, as sure as anything in history." The very exaggeration of this statement shows its bias. As sure as anything in history? It would be better to say that while nobody will ever know precisely what happened when Tone was held incommunicado by his captors after an illegal trial, there are few instances where suspicion is more justified, and historians are as entitled to record that Tone was murdered while in illegal custody, as to accept his jailors' word for it and record that he cut his own throat.

With the passing of Tone there perished the brightest mind of eighteenth century Ireland. The United Irishmen were not utterly extirpated as the rising of Robert Emmet five years later shows. But the world scene had shifted. No longer was the French revolution shedding the light of hope on all who dreamed of a better life. The Irish administration established in the glorious days of the American revolution was covered with ignominy and hatred at the conclusion of the French. It was only necessary now for Pitt to appear like Mephistopheles and claim his bond.

THE UNION

That bond was the Union. It must never be forgotten that the Union was not only aimed against Irish nationalism but against British democracy. The British oligarchy had been severely shaken by the wave of radicalism started by the two revolutions. The uniting of the British and Irish legislatures into one brought to Westminster 102 members, representing the landowners for the overwhelming part. The balance in favour of Toryism was so weighted as a result that parliamentary reform in England was delayed for a generation, namely until 1832.

To have attempted to bring Ireland into the Union before Irish Jacobinism had been crushed would have strengthened radicalism and hastened reform in Britain. But Britain dared not crush it herself. Hence Pitt's infamous policy of edging on the Irish government to every atrocity, skilfully affording the means while evading the responsibility, until in 1800 it was possible to appeal to the Catholics with promises of emancipation (immediately broken) and a seeming "way out" for all who were disgusted and dispirited and wanted a change.

The English landed and financial oligarchy strengthened itself against the rising industrial class by eliminating the danger of the French gaining a footing in Ireland. But the industrialists were compensated in that

105

Ireland was deprived of the power to legislate for the protection of her own industries. As was pointed out by T.A. Jackson,[7] the Union gave the appearance of fusing two nations; in fact it made their separation more marked. The "colonial" subordination of Ireland's economy to England was emphasised. The impact of the consequent national struggle now fell directly on the British Government. Ireland became a factor in British politics, and by the end of the century was the dominating factor.

CONCLUSION

The vision of Wolfe Tone was not fulfilled. The well-calculated effect of the Union was to break the alliance of Catholics and Dissenters, who did not attain complete emancipation until 1829, but came to depend not on the Irish Catholics but on the support of their co-religionists in Britain. But the Irish nation was now irrevocably formed. No longer was there a Gaeltacht and a Pale, a Catholic nation and a Protestant colony, but the people of Ireland now stood forth as one nation, divided not in point of religion or origin, but along the lines of class.

The ensuing period saw the struggle develop its new content with increasing sharpness. Ireland the nation was still a subject nation and struggled first for the repeal of the union, an issue incidentally taken up first by the Ulster Protestants. Secondly, since the landlords were increasingly exposed as the garrison class, the struggle developed for the ending of landlordism.

The first of these aims was achieved in 1921, the second, begun in the eighteen eighties, was completed in the twenties of this century. Throughout the period of the Union the creed of advanced nationalism spreading continuously through the body of the nation was Republicanism, which took on fresh significance with the rise of the working class, under the influence of Chartism, the International Workingmen's Association, and the Russian revolution, as at the hands of Mitchel, Lalor, Stephens, and Connolly.

Imperialism found new ways to thwart the will of the Irish people. Partition imposed from without an artificial division when the natural internal one had passed into history. The ranchers and "bondlords" replaced the landlords as the garrison class. The issues of the eighteenth century continued into the nineteenth in new forms; so those of the nineteenth continued in this century, also in new forms.

106

LEARN FROM TONE

It was the greatness of Tone, as Connolly remarked, that he "imitated no-body" but acted in accordance with the needs of the situation as he saw them. He did not construct the outlook of Republicanism out of nothing. He drew his conclusions from his own experience of life about him. He was pre-eminently practical despite his deep theoretical insight into the problems of his day. His autobiography and journals radiate the freshness of constant intellectual discovery, and he has the insuppressible gaiety of all truly dedicated men. In an age of giants he towered above all others. His epitaph is already written in the struggles and achievements of two centuries. He stands at the watershed of Irish nationalism, rejecting its rudimentary and announcing its classic form, and within the presentation of the Irish question as he learned to put it, is the germ of every issue that we are confronted with today.

But now there are advantages which Tone dared not even pray for. Instead of one transient revolutionary centre in France, there is a fixed world of anti-imperialist struggle. In place of the hesitant unity of a bourgeoisie whose parochialism repeatedly obstructed its universal objects, there is an Irish working class whose sole means of self-development lie in its unity, and whose interest demands the solidarity of workers everywhere. There is a powerfully organised British Labour movement whose interests are distinct from those of the bankers and bond-holders who are responsible for the partition and economic subjection of Ireland. The question before us today is whether a generation that has been bequeathed such advantages need fear failure in the work Wolfe Tone so boldly attempted in the "dark and evil days" of Fitzgibbon and Pitt. They need not fear provided they learn Tone's maxim of the unity of all those whose interest lies in the independence of Ireland.

References

1. J. Connolly, Labour in Irish History, Dublin 1956.
2. L. Morgan, Ancient Society, New York 1878.
3. G. B. O'Connor, Elizabethan Ireland, Dublin (no date).
4. D. A. Binchy, 'Secular Institutions' in M. Dillon (Ed.), Early Irish Society, Dublin 1959.
5. G. Thomson, Aeschylus and Athens, London 1939.
6. J. P. Prendergast, The Cromwellian Settlement of Ireland, Dublin 1922.
7. T. A. Jackson, Ireland Her Own, London 1947.
8. P. S. Dineen, Irish-English Dictionary, Dublin 1927.
9. R. Thurneysen, Grammar of Old Irish, Dublin 1946.
10. T. F. O'Rahilly, Early Irish History and Mythology, Dublin 1957.
11. P. S. O'Hegarty, History of Ireland under the Union, London 1952.
12. A. L. Morton, People's History of England, London 1938.
13. J. R. Green, Short History of the English People, London 1915.
14. A. S. Birnie, Economic History of the British Isles, London 1935.
15. A. S. Green, Henry the Second, London 1898.
16. G. Sigerson, Land Tenure and Land Classes in Ireland, Dublin 1871.
17. E. Spenser, View of the State of Ireland, 1595.
18. J. Davies, Discovery of the true causes why Ireland was never subdued, 1612.
19. A. Chichester, Proclamation of 11 March 1612.
20. R. N. Salaman, History and Social Influence of the Potato, Cambridge 1949.
21. J. S. Reid, History of the Presbyterian Church in Ireland, Belfast 1867.
22. T. Johnston, History of the working classes in Scotland, Glasgow c. 1923.
23. J. W. Good, Ulster and Ireland, Dublin 1919.
24. J. G. Leyburn, The Scotch-Irish, University of North Carolina Press,1963.
25 Haller and Davies, Leveller Tracts , New York 1944.
26. H. N. Brailsford, The Levellers, London 1961.
27. J. F. Taylor, Owen Roe O'Neill, Dublin 1891.
28. C. Petrie, The Jacobite Movement, London 1959.
29. J. Mitchel, History of Ireland, Glasgow 1876.
30. P. Harwood, History of the Irish Rebellion, London 1844.
31. J. Hely Hutchinson, Restraints on Irish Trade, reissued Dublin 1882.
32. S. G. Hobson, Irish Home Rule, Dublin 1912.
33. T. W. Tone, Argument on behalf of the Catholics of Ireland, Dublin 1791.
34. W. T. W. Tone, Life of Wolfe Tone, Washington, 1826.
35. B. O'Brien (Ed.), Autobiography of Wolfe Tone, London 1893.
36. B. O'Higgins, Wolfe Tone Annual, Dublin 1948.
37. A. de Blacam, Wolfe Tone, Dublin 1935.
38. D. Ireland, Patriot Adventurer, London 1936.
39. A. Milligan, Life of Wolfe Tone, Belfast 1898.
40. F. MacDermot, Theobald Wolfe Tone, London 1939.
41. R. R. Madden, Lives and Times of the United Irishmen, Dublin (series).
42. T. A. Jackson, Introduction to Essays on the French Revolution, London 1939.
43. A. L. Morton, The British Labour Movement 1770-1920, London 1956.

44. J. H. Rose, Revolutionary and Napoleonic Era 1789-1815, Cambridge 1919.
45. F. W. Chandler, Political Spies and Provocative Agents, Sheffield 1933.
46. S. Neilson (Ed.), Northern Star, Belfast. Files in National Library, Dublin.
47. E. Strauss, Irish Nationalism and British Democracy, London 1951.
48. D. A. Chart, Economic History of Ireland, Dublin 1920.
49. H. McNally, The Irish Militia 1793-1816, Dublin 1949.
50. "A member," History of Orangeism in Ireland, Belfast 1939.
51. Adoratsky (Ed.), Correspondence of Marx and Engels, London 1936.
52. B. Inglis, Freedom of the Press in Ireland 1784-1841, London 1946.
53. W. J. Fitzpatrick, The Sham Squire, Dublin 1895.
54. A. O'Connor, (Ed.), Irish Press, Dublin 1797. File in National Library, Dublin.
55. A. H. Dodd, Industrial Revolution in North Wales, Cardiff, 1933.
56. C. Dickson, The Wexford Rising in 1798, Tralee, 1956.